Churchill's Last Years

Churchill's Last Years

by ROY HOWELLS

DAVID McKAY COMPANY, INC.

New York

CHURCHILL'S LAST YEARS

Library of Congress Catalog Card Number: 66-13503

MANUFACTURED IN THE UNITED STATES OF AMERICA

VAN REES PRESS • NEW YORK

Contents

48529

Acknowledgment

I wish to thank Gerard Kemp for his extensive help and guidance in writing this book.

Foreword

There will always be a number of books published after the death of a very great man. Some of these will deal with high policy, others with the social aspects of his life, and yet others with the impact he made on the world in general.

This book is of quite another kind. It tries to give a picture of the purely domestic side of its subject by someone who was fortunate enough to be literally at his side for the last seven years of his life.

If one reads the memoirs of great men it is not always easy to form a complete picture when the smaller and more intimate details are missing. What did he do during the less important moments? What kind of a home did he live in? How did he cope with the lesser problems all of us have to face?

When a man becomes a legend in his own lifetime his essential humanity can become overlaid with the legend. Perhaps this chronicle of some remarkable years can fill in some of the gaps and let people today and in the years to come know another side of the life of that astonishing man, Sir Winston Spencer Churchill.

I

"How would you like to look after Sir Winston Churchill?"

EARLY in April 1958 Sir Winston Churchill had been desperately ill with pneumonia in the south of France. He was flown back to Britain and, as things turned out, it was to take him a full three months to recover properly from this setback. Naturally I saw his return reported in the newspapers but I had no idea that this event was to change the whole pattern of my life.

At the time I was looking after the elderly Scottish chairman of a large shipping line, and it was around midday on Saturday April 19th that his housekeeper told me that I was wanted on the telephone. The secretary of a London nursing agency was on the line. She got straight to the point.

"How would you like to look after Sir Winston Churchill?" she asked.

I took a deep breath as my head began to swim with the thought of the responsibility involved and the possible implications. She told me that my name had been put forward and that I would probably be needed for an interview. The agency advised me not to mention the job to anyone and said they would telephone me again later.

1

After a day's suspense I had a second phone call saying that an interview would not be necessary. A relief would be arranged for my Scottish patient if I would go down to Chartwell, in Kent, on April 27th to meet the Churchill family and assess what was involved. No contract had to be signed, the agency pointed out, and, in a complete daze, I found myself saying that naturally I would be very honored to take the job.

So, on the afternoon of the 27th, I caught the train from London to Westerham. All the way down to the country I sat staring out of the carriage window feeling very worried. I was having second thoughts about the enormous responsibility of what I was taking on. I knew of Churchill's bulldog spirit and wondered how I was expected to give such a man orders, for in nursing one sometimes has to lay down the law.

I had a Sunday newspaper on my lap but could not concentrate on it. As the fields and houses flashed by, the main thought running through my head was, "What is he really like—*now?*" I began to recall everything I had ever read about the man and realized that, no matter what impression other people had recorded, I was now going to be closer to him than anyone else alive. All I really knew about him was that he was probably the most famous man in the world and that he had led us to victory over Hitler. I think that I looked upon him more as a legend than as a real person.

The train pulled into Westerham station and I got off to find a chauffeur waiting with a hired car. He was Mr. Joe Jenner, Sir Winston's regular driver down at Chartwell. As we drove along the winding road from the station he warned me that Sir Winston was stern and demanding. He also said that he inspired loyalty and affection in all who worked for him. Jenner's advice accentuated my fears about what I was taking on. It was all rather forbidding. I was nervous and remained so for a long time afterward.

As the car turned through the main gates of Chartwell I caught my first glimpse of the place. Curiously, I was rather disappointed. I had imagined that Chartwell would be grand and imposing but I did not find it so from the front view. It was only later that I realized that the real beauty of Chartwell is seen from the rear of the house. The rolling lawns, the fishponds, the two lakes, the outdoor swimming pool, not tiled but so designed to blend beautifully with the surroundings, the fine trees standing in the meadows below the lawns, they all seem to epitomize the tranquil beauty of England and a gracious country home.

The car drew up at the policeman's lodge and I was met by Ivan Shepherd, the man I was to replace. He showed me round the house and pointed out my room, not far from Sir Winston's. The idea was for me to be close on hand in case of emergencies.

Shepherd outlined my duties and told me not to be nervous as we walked through the drawing room to meet Lady Churchill. She was writing letters, sitting at a desk with her back toward me. As she turned round my first impression was of a woman who looked much younger than her seventy-four years. After all, Sir Winston was then eighty-three and somehow I had imagined that his wife would look as elderly.

Lady Churchill took me along to see Sir Winston, who was reading in the study, sitting in a deep armchair. The study without him was imposing enough. The high ceiling had great oak beams and the walls were draped with flags; that of the Cinque Ports, of which he was Lord Warden, immediately caught the eye.

There was an enormous table covered with framed, signed photographs of many world-famous people and part of the walls was covered with scores of framed historic wartime messages, despatches and telegrams.

The most fascinating of these was the actual poster pinned up in Pretoria offering twenty-five pounds reward for Sir Winston "dead or alive" after his escape from a Boer prisoner of war camp; the poster had been given to him as a personal present. Among many paintings and drawings in the study were two pencil sketches of him drawn by his daughter, Sarah. One was a back view, very well done, bringing out the bulk and stoop of the man; the other, a profile, unmistakably Sir Winston. The sketches hung either side of the huge open fireplace. Above it was a large painting of Lord Randolph Churchill, Sir Winston's father, sitting at his writing table, which stood by the window.

Another of the paintings on the walls was of a black and white bulldog, really a symbolic picture of Sir Winston. Above this again hung a pen-and-ink portrait of Bernard Baruch, a life-long American friend. A large part of two walls was lined with books, many of them leather-bound complete sets.

Standing on a chest, all in small, delicate frames, were photographs of Lady Churchill, the Queen, and Sir Winston's daughters in various uniforms. On the writing table stood two other pictures: his mother and father. These were painted on enamel plaques set in oval leather cases. A large piece of shrapnel mounted on a metal base was on the window sill. It was presented to Sir Winston by Lord Montgomery and I believe it was a piece of shrapnel that had just missed him during the war.

The armchair had loose fawn covers, I remember. I had expected a great leather armchair and was somehow disappointed not to find him buried in one. Small details tend to stick in the mind, and the loose covers came as a surprise. He was wearing glasses and drinking brandy and

4

soda. His cigar was in the ashtray, the smoke curling up to the beamed ceiling.

Our introduction was simple in the extreme. "Winston dear," said Lady Churchill, "this is Mr. Howells. He's come to help look after you."

Sir Winston remained where he was and took my outstretched hand. Immediately he got my name wrong and he never got it right all the time I was with him. "How do you do, Howes," he said.

I found myself dry-mouthed but managed to croak out, "Good afternoon, sir." It was quite an ordeal. Sir Winston stared hard at me and I was completely overawed. All I could think of was that he did not look eighty-three. I would have said that at that time he looked in his early seventies.

His cherub-like pink face was the kind that defied the years. He was white-haired, I noticed, and going thin on top. As he stared hard at me it was as if he was weighing me up on the spot. I felt he was thinking: "You surely don't think a young chap like you is going to be able to cope with *me,* do you?" Secretly I hoped someone would come in and take me away, saying it had all been a mistake and that I was not to have the job.

However, Shepherd eventually returned and told Sir Winston that he would show me over the rest of the house. Automatically I gave a nervous half bow and walked out of the room.

I went on duty that night. Shepherd said, "It's a bit nerve-wracking at first, but once you settle down to him he's not so bad." He dropped a hint that although I was hired to look after Sir Winston, really as an insurance against illness rather than any specific nursing, I would find myself doing a variety of jobs for him.

I could not get over the fact that I was going to be with the greatest living Englishman. I was rather an independent person myself and wondered exactly how it was all going to work out.

I had arrived in London in 1953 with five shillings in my pocket to take a three-year nursing course at Dulwich Hospital. Apart from my two years of National Service, it was the first time I had been away from my Welsh home in Haverfordwest, Pembrokeshire.

My salary during the training period was practically non-existent, amounting to about six dollars a week. Although I loved the hospital work, I found it impossible to continue once I had qualified.

So I left and became a personal nurse. There were lean times with periods of no work at all. And when I did work I occasionally had difficulty in obtaining my wages!

Gradually I learned that relatives of my patients were sending in good reports about me to the nursing agency; so much so that eventually I found myself looking after Mayfair patients.

I later discovered that Lady Churchill had been to the agency, which had strongly recommended me for the post of looking after her husband. It was a tremendous honor.

But before I go any further, let me give a brief impression of Chartwell. As I have said, it is at first sight a rather nondescript building when seen from the front, with a short drive up to the entrance. As you enter the heavy oak front door with its two brass rings, you find yourself in a small porch. Double clear-glass doors lead into the hall, which contains a long low oak chest for hats and rugs. A large, ornate gold clock stands on the chest alongside a leather-bound visitors' book, closed with a lock.

Hanging on the wall immediately above the chest is Sir Winston's famous oil painting of bottles, once referred to as a "bottlescape." One might have expected the hall to contain armor and swords and pikes on the walls. But the plaster walls are lined with none of these things, and the

6

only ancient military relics in Chartwell are upstairs in the study: a shield at the center of a display of old weapons.

The only room off the hall is Lady Churchill's large bedroom opening onto her dressing room. Stairs, fitted with light blue carpet, lead up to the first floor and down to the basement cinema and wine cellar. Turning left at the top of the hall, one finds oneself in a small corridor, which leads to the library and the drawing room. The library contains a huge relief map of the D-Day Normandy landings set in a glass case and stretching the length of one wall. It is built in fantastic detail even down to tiny landing barges.

There is a television set, a writing table, and two heavy armchairs, and only the book-lined walls relieve it of austerity.

If the library is essentially Sir Winston in atmosphere, then the drawing room very much reflects Lady Churchill's character. It is a very long elegant room, beautifully decorated in primrose, the floor covered by enormous Persian carpets. It is light, roomy, and very feminine.

To the left of the drawing room is a specially installed elevator and leading from it are two rooms, used by the secretarial staff and containing the switchboard and an enormous display of signed photographs of all the generals in the Second World War. Hanging with them are framed original drawings by David Low, the cartoonist.

At the top of the stairs on the first floor stands a three-foot-high black iron lion. Every time Sir Winston passed it he used to pat its head fondly. Along the corridor are the main guest bedroom, the dining room and two other guest rooms, the Brown Room and the Green Room. Along the walls of the first-floor corridor hang six of Sir Winston's oil paintings, all illuminated by small individual lights.

His bedroom is very small and very austere; just a large double bed against the wall in the corner, Persian rugs

7

covering a scrubbed white-wood floor, a bay window over-looking the orchard and croquet lawn, and a unique collapsible dressing table built into the window. At the pull of a cord, a mirror slides up from a wooden casing and so the dressing table is really a wooden flap, erected rather like setting up half a gateleg table.

To the right of the bay window is the bathroom containing an enormous sunken bath. Sir Winston loved his two baths a day and always enjoyed wallowing about, using an outsize sponge.

In his later years he used to play a curiously boyish trick in the bath. He would take the sponge, hold it over his face, and slowly sink under the water. This used to give everyone a rather worrying time but he always surfaced, beaming and delightfully pink.

He slept with one pillow and had a second one alongside his body. It was there as a marker, the idea being that if he woke in the night, he would know exactly how far he was from the edge of the bed.

On the second floor is another guest room, called the Tower Room, the remaining rooms being taken up by the staff. At the back of the house are immaculately kept lawns, rhododendron bushes and, to the left, a rose garden and summer house, the walls of which are decorated by murals by John Spencer Churchill, depicting the Battle of Blenheim. The summer house has unusual carvings set in its walls: heads of William of Orange; Queen Anne; Marlborough, Sir Winston's great ancestor; and Sarah, his duchess.

A path leads through the rose garden down to the fishponds, the swimming pool, and two lakes, one of which has an island in the middle reached by a wooden bridge. On the other side of the house is the croquet lawn leading to the kitchen garden, the orchard, and Sir Winston's studio.

I had just two days at Chartwell before I was introduced

to the peculiar system of switching between there and the family home at Hyde Park Gate in London. It was quite an upheaval the first time and remained so throughout. This was the plan: an estate car was loaded up with suitcases, hatboxes, garden produce, fresh flowers, and set off in advance. Then there was another big car to take the cook, housemaid, lady's maid, kitchenmaid, butler. And a third to take Sir Winston and Lady Churchill. A fourth car carried the secretary on duty, myself, boxes of private papers, and anything that might have been left behind in the rush.

Every Tuesday and Friday I always went to bed completely exhausted after the changeover, and I never really got used to the fact that Sir Winston always seemed to delay his departure. If he was in bed, he always stayed there until the last minute. If he was in the garden, he always insisted upon sitting in the fresh air. I was left tearing round in circles, throwing things into suitcases and rushing to get everything into the last car. Because Sir Winston liked to find the same things in their place in his bedroom no matter where he was, we always had the job of transferring every item in the bedroom from one house to the other, even down to the ashtrays. The amazing thing was that items were rarely, if ever, left behind.

That first week, Sir Winston had his first night out since his illness. This was the Royal Academy dinner at Burlington House, Piccadilly. Before the dinner he toured the galleries, which held three of his own paintings. One of them was "Oranges and Lemons," finished in the south of France only a few days before his illness.

It was the kind of evening Sir Winston relished. Old political friends and colleagues were there to meet him. Lord Attlee, Lord Halifax, Lord Swinton, and Viscount Samuel. The Academy president, Sir Charles Wheeler, sat at Sir Winston's side. He frequently visited him at Chartwell, discussing painting and techniques in Sir Winston's spacious studio, which stood a couple of hundred yards away from the house among the trees in the orchard.

For the occasion Sir Winston wore the blue sash and star of the Order of the Garter and all his medals. He was always impatient when being dressed up for big occasions like this, usually muttering away to himself as I helped him into his clothes.

As I pinned on his Order of Merit, which hung from a ribbon around his neck, I asked, "Does that look right?"

He replied curtly, "Well, *I* don't know. Don't you?"

I had never dressed anyone for such an occasion before, and felt a little nervous. Somehow I had been under the impression that a valet would be brought in to dress him. After all, I had been taken on as a personal nurse.

It was the first indication that the job was to be something more than nursing. Realizing that I was to be responsible for making sure Sir Winston was correctly turned out for the dinner, I quickly checked to find photographs of him wearing his decorations. An old cover picture from *Life* magazine came in very handy as a guide.

By the time I had finished, he had an amazing number of gold safety pins in his evening dress. Then a terrible thought struck me. "You won't be taking your coat off, will you?" I asked.

Sir Winston chuckled, obviously regarding that as a big joke. "I think not," he replied.

There were two safety pins on his trouser hip to hold the blue sash and two more holding it in position in the small of his back. Then there were two others keeping the Order of Merit in position, one pinning down the white waistcoat at the back, and yet another holding his ready-made white bow tie.

Sir Winston did not mind the gold safety pins as long as he looked all right. I often thought to myself as I saw him leave for such an important function, "It's a good thing no one knows about all those pins."

He was the most impossible, arrogant, yet lovable and wonderful patient imaginable. All the time I was with him I knew I was in the presence of greatness, yet I saw him in an entirely different light from everyone else. It was as if I was studying the greatest man of the century through a giant magnifying glass. I was so close to him that I feel as if I have lived with history and at the closest possible quarters. I saw him not as so many others did, through rose-colored glasses, but as he really was.

I saw every side of the Churchill character, day in, day out. Every mood, every change of expression. It did not take long to realize the loyalty he inspired, yet his personality was, at times, completely overwhelming. He drained the people around him of every last drop of energy and there was never a day when I came off duty without feeling completely all in. Apart from the physical strain, the mental wear and tear was tremendous. For he inspired a curious love-hate relationship in those under him, so that one loved him part of the time, hated him part of the time, yet liked him all the time.

I soon discovered that he had very definite ideas about sleeping. He used to turn in around midnight and expect me to do the same about an hour later. The reason for this was that he did not like to see people fully dressed in the middle of the night. "Everyone should sleep at night," he used to say.

When I first joined him, he was using a black satin mask tied with elastic at the back of his head. It was to shield his eyes on waking, and he used to put it on the last thing before turning out his bedside light. Before I joined him he used the mask during the daytime because it helped him snatch a few minutes' sleep, especially when he was in cars or planes. These continual cat naps undoubtedly helped him during the war years when his energies were at full stretch. The mask was essential.

In later years, however, I noticed that he stopped wearing it. This may have had something to do with his eyesight, which seemed to improve with age. He used to wear glasses for reading when I first joined him but after a few years his eyesight improved and he was able to read without glasses.

Every morning he had breakfast in bed, usually a cooked meal: steak, bacon and eggs, fresh salmon occasionally. He followed it with coffee, toast and, strangely enough, jam. He always insisted on jam for breakfast, disliking marmalade. Black cherry jam was his favorite. If the jam was not there he would wait until it was brought in. He was most particular about small details like this. Another thing he was fussy about was his morning bath. He would not get in unless the water was at 98° F., staring at the bath thermometer every time to make sure it was on the mark. Once in, he used to insist on more hot water being added until the bath thermometer registered 104° F.

I would walk into the bedroom each morning, draw back the curtains, and wait to see how he reacted to my greeting.

If he was in a good mood he would reply in a rather staccato manner: "Good morning. What sort of day?" Then everything would proceed smoothly.

But if he was out of sorts, my cheerful "Good morning" would be greeted either by stony silence or a grunt, and he would not even bother to open his eyes.

Routine in the mornings was always the same. A small black poodle belonging to Lady Churchill's secretary would trot into the bedroom and jump onto the bed.

There it would wait until Sir Winston gave it two lumps of sugar. Once that little ritual was over, he would have breakfast off his tray, tackling the morning papers at the same time. He usually started with *The Times,* always placed on top of the pile, and worked his way through until he reached the *Daily Worker* at the bottom. He tackled the leaders first. Frequently he became so engrossed in his reading that he would get his black cherry jam all over the bottom half of the newspapers with the result that the pages stuck together. It was often one of my lesser duties to remove the jam.

As he finished reading each newspaper he would let it drop so that it slid off the counterpane onto the floor. By the time he had got through the pile, the bed was surrounded by crumpled papers. He spent two hours every morning in this way. At first I used to pick up the newspapers when he dropped them, but soon learned that he always did this and no amount of tidying up after him made any difference.

He never commented about things he read in the newspapers. He just ploughed on through them silently, making sure he read the financial columns and the horseracing news. Sometimes he handed me part of the newspaper, pointing to an article, saying, "Keep that for me." The article would be put on his bedside table until he needed it again. Usually he kept the items to show friends or members of the family.

He subscribed to a clipping agency, which sent him any newspaper story mentioning his name, and one morning when I returned from a day off he had something for me. He held out a snippet of paper and said, "I just thought you might like to have this."

I saw that the story was taken from my hometown newspaper in Wales. They had discovered that I was working for Sir Winston and had given me a write-up in their gossip column.

"I'm sorry about this, Sir Winston," I said. "I try to avoid this kind of thing."

13

He just smiled, waved his hands and said, "These things are unavoidable. You are not to blame."

Sir Winston seemed to worry far less about matters of this nature than others in the household.

There were days when he wanted to dictate a letter as soon as he woke. I remember one occasion. He called me and said, "Ask her to come up," meaning the girl secretary. The minutes ticked by and he became impatient.

"Where is she?" he asked. "Where's the girl gone?"

I explained that the secretary was not yet on duty. But it did not really satisfy him. I went to great lengths to point out that she had set hours. It made no difference to Sir Winston.

"This is monstrous!" he roared. "WHY isn't she here? She *should* be here. I can't understand what is going on."

It probably stemmed from the war years when Sir Winston had a secretary at his beck and call twenty-four hours a day. He never really understood why she was not always readily available.

He was very impatient over things like this. If he rang his bell, he expected someone to appear almost immediately, rather like a genie answering the summons of a magic lamp.

When the girl secretary arrived, he asked her accusingly: "Where have you been?"

She started to explain but he cut her short with, "Come along now. I want you to take a letter."

After dictating, he smiled disarmingly and said sweetly, "Thank you, my dear."

One of the toughest jobs was getting Sir Winston out of bed in the mornings. He had to be up for lunch at 1:15 P.M. and practically every time he was late. Whenever this happened he became furious and blamed me. We tried all kinds of ruses to get him out of bed in time, one of them was setting forward every clock in his bedroom.

We tried this too often, however, and eventually he became wise to it. I spotted him one day checking the bedroom clocks against his pocket watch. In an attempt to beat this maneuver, I countered by putting his pocket watch ten minutes ahead when he was not looking. Still he was suspicious. He used to win in the end by asking someone entering the room, no matter how many clocks he had around him, "Uh-huh, what *time* is it?" The person naturally told the truth, and we were back where we started.

All this time I was with him he was consistently unpunctual, always fuming with annoyance whenever I tried to hurry him, and no amount of coaxing on my part had any effect. Yet he expected everything and everyone to be in place on time, particularly if he was going out.

It seems rather ironic that earlier in his life unpunctuality had been something he deplored. Indeed, he once described it as "a vile habit." Nevertheless I believe it had always been one of his weaknesses and one he never successfully conquered.

The London house was actually two houses in one: 27 and 28 Hyde Park Gate, a quiet little cul-de-sac not far from the Albert Hall and five minutes' walk from Kensington Gardens.

The black front door with its large silver knocker opens onto a small porch similar to the one at Chartwell except that here there are four steps up to the glass doors especially put in to keep out draft. In the hall, fitted with blue carpeting, stands a long wooden stand holding rugs. On top of the stand is a bronze model of a racehorse and at its side a knee-high ornamental vase with a goodly collection of walking sticks, umbrellas, parasols, and shooting sticks.

On the opposite wall, above a radiator, hang two pictures, prints of a Court scene and of the Chamber of the

House of Commons, both dating back to Queen Anne's reign.

Walking from the hall down the main corridor, the first room one saw on the right was Sir Winston's drawing room, large and long with a most striking painting of Sir Winston hanging above a small writing bureau. The portrait is by the late Sir Oswald Birley, one of Sir Winston's great friends. He painted him, head and shoulders, wearing one of his famous wartime siren suits. On the same wall farther down the room hangs another Birley painting, a portrait in oils of Sir Winston's youngest daughter, Mary Soames.

At both ends of the room stand bookcases filled with hundreds of leather-bound volumes. Paintings of the Duke of Marlborough, and his wife Sarah, hang on either side of the fireplace, above which is another old print; the whole room is a beautiful blend of old and new. Of all the rooms in Sir Winston's London and Chartwell homes it was the one I found the most striking.

This is the room where the family used to gather for a drink before lunch and dinner. Sir Winston always sat on the left of the fireplace in the same armchair, a rather small chair with faded pink loose covers. Lady Churchill would sit opposite her husband in a similar chair but with a high, straight back and side wings. When the family were there, they would group themselves in an arc between these two chairs, stretching their legs out in front of the log fire. Sir Winston always had a small side table next to him for his cigars, matches, and brandy. From time to time the butler, Enrique, a dark-haired Spaniard, would step forward with a log to build up the fire, which Lady Churchill insisted should be kept going all day whenever Sir Winston was in the house. The fires used to burn summer and winter; frequently the drawing room was more like a Turkish bath because there were also two radiators under the windows and often there were as many as eight huge logs blazing

16

away in the fireplace. Up to a few years before he died, Sir Winston used to throw the logs on himself. He would take them off the pile at the side of the hearth and toss them on one-handed. When, toward the end of his life, he could no longer manage it, he used to prod them with his walking stick, sometimes using the hook to drag them along. This would bring a stern reproof from Lady Churchill.

The drawing room ran the full width of the house with windows at one end looking out onto the street and opening onto the garden at the other end.

Immediately opposite the drawing room was a corridor connecting the house with Number 27, originally used purely as offices. After Sir Winston's fall in 1962, the largest room in Number 27 was redecorated as his bedroom.

This was the room he died in. Two built-in wardrobes faced his bed, and joining them was a long cupboard with a flat formica top that served as a dressing table. A large mirror was screwed to the wall over this table, which held a gold cup won by one of his horses and two china lovebirds given him as a birthday present by his wife. Immediately above the mirror was one of his many seascapes.

Sir Winston's bed was identical to the one he had at Chartwell, almost as broad as it was long. It was an extremely heavy bed. I know because I once had to take it to pieces. This happened during the winter of 1963 when a main fuse blew in that half of the house. It was late at night and the electrician could not come till the next morning. Rather than risk my patient sleeping in an unheated room, we decided to dismantle his bed and move it to the reception room in Number 28, which was on a different circuit. Sir Winston could not understand why he could not sleep in his bedroom as usual with extra blankets. He was quite adamant about this when he saw that his bed had been moved and it looked for a time as if the bed would have to be taken down again and returned. But eventually he was persuaded that he would be better off in the reception room, and there he stayed the night. The next morning he insisted on getting up at 10 A.M., most unusual because he normally never rose before midday. He dressed and stumped off to the drawing room until the electrician called and the bed was put back.

Immediately above his pillow hung a large painting of the House of Commons viewed from the River Thames. At the side of his bed was a long glass-topped table holding an angle-poised lamp, a gold clock presented to him by Lord Beaverbrook, his gold pocket watch, hair brushes, a small gold box containing toothpicks, a large wooden box containing an assortment of cigars, and a pile of books from Kensington Public Library. Underneath the table would be his black leather-bound despatch box, which went everywhere with him. It contained all his personal papers and could only be opened with one key, which hung on his watch chain.

On either side of the bed hung paintings of the Jeromes of New York, his maternal grandparents. An enormous writing table stood near the large bay window and on top of this was a lamp with a large red shade.

A silver framed photograph of Lady Churchill stood in front of the lamp. It showed her wearing a flowered hat tilted well over her forehead. This was one of his favorite photographs of his wife and he used it as a guide when he painted her portrait, which still hangs in the Chartwell studio.

Outside the bedroom, across the corridor, was a small anteroom and next to this was his bathroom with its safety rails along the walls. A long brass handrail ran along the corridor to the drawing room, but although this was fitted after his fall he rarely used it. Typically, he deliberately chose to ignore it, preferring instead to manage with his walking stick.

I never ceased to wonder at Sir Winston's tremendous courage in the last years of his life. It would have been so easy for him to give up and rely solely on the wheelchair that was always available. After all, he had suffered four strokes and had lost a certain amount of movement on both sides of his body. But he overcame physical handicaps by sheer determination. It was never more in evidence than when walking from his bedroom to join guests in the drawing room.

Whenever he had to do this I always walked one pace behind in case he stumbled. I remember how he used to walk the length of the corridor leaning on his stick and then, just as he was about to turn into the drawing room, visibly brace himself, throwing back his shoulders to stride in to meet his guests. He also did this when leaving the house to get into his car. He knew a small crowd would be waiting outside and I am sure he was determined to show them that he was far from being a senile old man. He was fully aware that some people had written him off because of his age but he was too great a man to allow this to affect him in any way.

Just across the hall at his London home is his very unusual dining room. It is on a different floor. One walked through the dining-room door and across a gallery with a balustrade, looking down into the dining room as one might look down on a stage. Three Chinese idols stood in illuminated alcoves halfway down the small curved staircase. The table in the middle of the room is of white wood, well scrubbed like a farmhouse table. Above the open fireplace hangs a painting of Marlborough receiving the surrender of Marshal Tallard at the Battle of Blenheim. Near this hang portraits of the Duke of Wellington and the Duke of Marlborough.

Two painted metal elephants stand on either side of the fireplace. They were gifts from Aristotle Onassis, presented

19

after Sir Winston had admired a similar pair on board his yacht. One of Sir Winston's own paintings is on the opposite wall: a peaceful picture of the fishponds at Chartwell showing the golden orfe. He was very fond of this because it reminded him of his country home.

A luggage elevator had been converted for use between the gallery and the dining room. It was carefully designed so that it blended in perfectly with the rest of the room and the elevator base was made of wood cut from the dining-room floor.

The whole room is light and airy with two enormous windows opening out onto the small garden. This is beautifully kept by the part-time gardener and has flowers in bloom for much of the year. The lawn is surrounded by a paved pathway, and sometimes Sir Winston would sit out in a wicker chair, his legs wrapped in a rug, a heavy coat on his shoulders and his huge Stetson on his head. He frequently used to point across the lawn to a patch of sunlight in the late afternoon and say, "I'd like to go over there." With the butler I used to lift him in his chair and carry him across. Once or twice, when there was no one available, I pulled him in the chair across the lawn, scoring the turf. Afterward I surreptitiously stamped down the divots and made sure I avoided the gardener for the next few days.

II

On the Riviera

THREE months after joining Sir Winston I was told that he intended spending the summer in the south of France. Although I knew of his trips to the Riviera each summer, I somehow had not anticipated that I would be included in the party. And when Mr. Anthony Montague Browne, his secretary, broke the news to me, I found myself totally unprepared for such a trip. My means were limited, and I had a very meager wardrobe indeed. But nothing was said about outfitting me with the kind of clothes people wore on the Riviera, and I had the feeling, rightly or wrongly, that Sir Winston and Lady Churchill never realized that I might be in this predicament.

I rushed out and spent a week's salary on a pair of slacks and some shirts. As it turned out, when I got to the south of France I found that the more money people had, the less attention they paid to their dress. It seemed as if I had suddenly been plunged into a dream world.

The Churchills were guests of Lord Beaverbrook at his beautiful white villa, La Capponcina, at Cap d'Ail. It was a glorious summer, eight weeks of continuous sunshine, which I was able to enjoy to the full.

When I arrived at Nice airport I was completely lost until I noticed a uniformed chauffeur standing by the Customs office holding up a small white card on which my name was printed. I walked across, pointed to the card, then at myself. I spoke little French. He picked up my luggage and disappeared into the crowd with me following. We got into the waiting car and I was then driven off at a hair-raising speed through Nice and on toward Monte Carlo.

We were doing about sixty miles an hour and I must confess that, as the road is a long series of sharp bends with a sheer drop on one side, I was more interested in the driver's ability to keep the car on the road than in the scenery.

The car turned off the main road in the middle of the village of Cap d'Ail, went down a narrow road toward the sea, and suddenly swung left through some high wooden-studded gates set in a long stone wall. We were at the villa. It looked like something out of a film, secluded, and surrounded by hundreds of tropical plants, flowers and bushes. My first impressions were of a patio, a fountain playing, bunches of small grapes hanging from latticework, and an outdoor green-tiled swimming pool. I was shown round by one of the staff and then taken in the car to a small hotel a hundred yards away where I was to stay.

They were unforgettable days. Everywhere Sir Winston went he had a fantastic reception. The French people loved him. Indeed, they had made him honorary mayor of Cap d'Ail six years earlier. But each time I think of those holidays my mind goes back to one woman, Greta Garbo. It was during that summer of 1958 that he met her for the first time. Her villa was only half a mile down the coast, and as she often dined with Lord Beaverbrook, he invited her to La Capponcina during Sir Winston's visit.

I will never forget the night they met. Lord Beaverbrook gave a special dinner party to mark the occasion, also inviting Sir Winston's old friend Aristotle Onassis and his wife Tina. All my life I had worshipped Garbo as a screen actress and so apparently had Sir Winston. When she walked into the salon to meet him, she seemed rather smaller than I had expected. Immediately they struck up a genuine friendship. Sir Winston loved being in the company of beautiful women and certainly Garbo is among the most beautiful in the world.

He had seen all her films in the basement cinema at Chartwell, and after their first meeting that August they frequently dined together whenever Sir Winston was on the Riviera. Sometimes it was at the Chateau de Madrid restaurant, and at others, on board Onassis' yacht *Christina* in Monaco harbor.

Over roast duck, Sir Winston asked Garbo not to hide herself from the world and to return to the screen once more. She appeared flattered at the suggestion, and for a time there was talk of her playing a nun in a film to be made in France. She was at that time fifty-two, but her facial bone structure was such that she still retained the mysterious beauty that had made her famous.

It was while Sir Winston and Lady Churchill were staying at Lord Beaverbrook's villa that summer that they celebrated their golden wedding anniversary, on September 12. It coincided with a rather special present from France, the Medaille de la Courtoisie Française. The medal was to mark Sir Winston's services to France, and it was a fitting tribute to the man who, in the dark days of 1940, made the inspiring offer to all Frenchmen to become equal citizens of the British Commonwealth. The award was made by the French Academician Jean Cocteau, the author and poet, who lived on the Riviera. He prepared an eloquent address in French for the occasion, which was celebrated with a family party in the main grounds of Beaverbrook's villa.

Four days before the celebration Sir Winston and Lady Churchill drove into Nice for a special dinner in their honor given by the Prefect of the Alpes-Maritimes Department, M. Pierre-Jean Moatti. It was only one of many celebrations that week to mark the great occasion. I remember the shoals of presents arriving at the villa and the hundreds of messages and telegrams the postmen delivered by the sackful. Several amateur artists sent Sir Winston their paintings, a champagne firm sent a dozen bottles of its finest vintage. The gifts came from all over the world.

The family all flew out from England and it was not until we returned home that we were to see their present, a magnificent rose garden, specially laid out in the grounds of Chartwell.

It was, I understand, the idea of Sir Winston's son, Randolph. He suggested an avenue of golden roses to his sisters and they agreed. The roses could not be planted until late October, and it was Mary Soames who thought that in the meantime they should present their parents with a large illuminated book, incorporating a dedication, the design of the avenue, and a list of the twenty-eight varieties of rose that were to be planted. Someone suggested embellishing the book with individual pictures of the roses painted by leading flower painters, and work was carried out in the remarkably short time of four weeks.

Among the artists were Augustus John, Mr. R. A. Butler (then Home Secretary), Ivon Hitchens, Duncan Grant, Cecil Beaton, John Nash, Oliver Messel and, adding a family flavor, Betty Churchill, the widow of Lord Ivor Churchill. A blank page was specially inserted at the end for Sir Winston to add his own rose picture. Randolph was in charge of sending out the roses to the artists, and the book was kept as a complete surprise until his daughter

Arabella, a pretty young woman who wore her long hair rather like Alice in Wonderland, handed it over at the family party. The strangest thing about the whole business of the present was that it was planted in the kitchen garden, flanked by strawberry beds on one side and rows of cabbages on the other.

Sir Winston was a man of routine and the whole of that wonderful summer on the Riviera he took his usual two baths a day. He always did this no matter where he was. The bathroom at Lord Beaverbrook's villa had a large window of frosted glass taking up the best part of one wall, and when the light was on in the bathroom, it attracted the night moths that fluttered against the windowpane.

Lizards, common in the south of France, would lurk round the sides of the window before crawling out to stalk and pick off the moths. I remember Sir Winston lying in his bath at night, watching the lizards chew up their victims. He gritted his teeth and winced at the gruesome exhibition, but when I suggested tapping on the window to frighten the lizards away, he was against it.

During the day Sir Winston spent his time on the terrace, reading all the English newspapers, which had been specially flown out. Although he loved the sun, he never sunbathed. Always he wore his broad-brimmed Stetson hat with the brim turned down in front to shade his eyes. He had sunglasses but rarely, if ever, wore them. He liked to see the colors around him as they really were; he could not bear to see the bright blues, greens, yellows, and reds of the Riviera toned down.

Lady Churchill sat outside with her husband, with a parasol to ward off the hot sun. Even at seventy-four she had a wonderful complexion, one that was to last. It was probably partly due to her fitness, for she went swimming in the sea off the private beach with Lady Birley, Sir

Oswald Birley's widow. She used the breast stroke and was quite a good swimmer, slipping into her costume in the villa and walking down to the beach in a robe and an unusual bathing cap, rather in the style of a Victorian maid's mop cap. Sir Winston had his swimming trunks with him and practically every morning announced, "I'm going for a swim today." This used to cause widespread panic among the staff, who then had the job of dissuading him. Dr. David Roberts, his physician in the south of France, sometimes had to be called in to lay down the law if Sir Winston could not be persuaded that at eighty-four, and after his attack of pneumonia the previous spring, he would be ill advised to go into the water. We were not so much worried about getting him into the water; it was the business of getting him out. But he never gave up. Every day of our stay at the village he tried and failed to get his swim.

He was always looking for allies after Dr. Roberts turned him down. Someone, anyone, who would back him up and say, "Yes, Sir Winston, I think a swim would do you good."

One afternoon, having sounded out everyone from Lady Churchill down to sundry secretaries, he turned to me and said: "Do *you* think I should be allowed to swim?"

I replied that I thought it might be unwise.

"Rubbish!" he roared.

To round off the summer holiday that year, Onassis invited Sir Winston and Lady Churchill on board his yacht, the *Christina,* for a ten-day cruise, and the yacht's lockers were specially stocked with everything Sir Winston liked. Winston junior, then seventeen, was among the guests, who also included Maria Callas and her husband. The yacht called at Majorca and Cartagena before arriving at Gibraltar, where Sir Winston drove through cheering crowds, giving the V-for-Victory sign and later going to feed the apes on the Rock. During the war he had given special orders that apes were to be smuggled into Gibraltar as their numbers were diminishing. There was an old belief that if they left the Rock, the British would, too.

On board the yacht the usual card games were played. Bezique was the favorite, and each time the cards came out so did Sir Winston's special green velvet table cover, which he took everywhere. For some reason he also took with him a maroon cover. It was widely reported at the time that Onassis and his guests played for high stakes but in actual fact it was only a penny a point.

The yacht *Christina* was really a converted British frigate. Onassis bought twenty-four of them to use as a whaling fleet, later selling all but one. He had his own red and white seaplane parked on the yacht's stern and his car, a mini-runabout, was stowed on the lower deck. The crew were Greeks, with a German wireless operator who used to prepare and type out special news bulletins, which were given to the guests. The seaplane pilot was not a regular member of the crew but came aboard whenever Onassis had a business appointment and needed to fly away from the yacht cruise for a few days.

On these trips Sir Winston always wore his favorite yachting cap, that of an Elder Brother of Trinity House. He was a strong believer in dressing correctly for all occasions. This was a curious side to his character, the love of dressing up. His wardrobe at Hyde Park Gate contained every conceivable uniform and dress needed for every conceivable occasion.

Onassis' yacht was extremely luxurious, even down to the gold bath taps made in the form of dolphins. It had its own small hospital and a laundry run by a Greek husband and wife who managed to do dry cleaning in record time. There were telephones in every bedroom, each of which had its own bathroom. Air-conditioning was fitted throughout and the owner had gone to enormous expense to have installed a Cretan mosaic dance floor that would convert at the touch of a switch to a swimming pool. The salon had gold and silver ashtrays in the form of sea shells, and the salon centerpiece was one of Sir Winston's landscapes. The whole of the yacht was breathtaking; I never ceased to wonder at the opulence that surrounded me.

Every evening Onassis and his guests saw a film on board. "Sea Wolf," an adventure thriller, and Jayne Mansfield's pictures were among Sir Winston's favorites that summer.

Strangely enough the yacht, with all its gadgets, had only one film projector. This meant that at the end of every reel there was a short interval while the new reel was put on. A general discussion about the film used to ensue and any parts that Sir Winston had missed, or could not understand, were filled in by his host. The films went on until about midnight, everyone usually turning in at about 1 A.M.

Onassis and Sir Winston got on wonderfully well together. The Greek millionaire shipowner was extremely kind to his guest and went out of his way to make sure that he had everything he wanted and was well entertained.

Some days Onassis would ask Sir Winston, "What would you feel like doing today, sir?" He never called his guest "Winston." It was either "sir" or "Sir Winston."

From the depths of his wicker basket chair on the poop deck would come the reply, "I don't really mind."

Sir Winston meant it. He was quite happy to sit there admiring the Mediterranean scenery, some of which was breathtaking.

Onassis would say, "There's a very nice little island which I visited last year and which I wouldn't mind seeing again."

His guest replied, "Yes, I would like that very much."

That was the kind of conversation that passed between the two. Onassis, unlike many people around the great man, never said things like, "I feel you would like so-and-so" or "Don't you think you should do this?" He invariably came up with a direct suggestion and left it to his guest to make the next move.

Sir Winston never enthused over things and places seen on the cruise. He enjoyed them but quietly. People who did not know him would not have detected this.

The days quickly passed by, much of the time being spent relaxing on deck. The more energetic guests would swim, but Onassis was usually to be found sitting on the deck crosslegged near Sir Winston's chair, listening to his views. There were always drinks at hand, and Onassis used to take considerable pride in the cocktails he made in the bar of his yacht.

One afternoon I was in the bar when he walked in. He asked me, "What are you drinking?" I told him that I usually stuck to gin and tonic. He said, "Try this." He then concocted a drink for me while I looked on rather apprehensively. It was a tricky situation. I wondered: should I accept and drink, or refuse and risk slighting him? I decided to take the glass, holding it, I must confess, rather gingerly.

I took one sip. It rocked me to the heels. The cocktail was just about the strongest thing I have ever tasted. I still have no idea what he put in it.

Onassis simply smiled and left to rejoin Sir Winston after topping up his own glass. He had a lively sense of humor and one that was in complete contrast to that of his guest. Sir Winston's humor was always dry. In fact I am sure that there must have been times when people were unsure whether he was joking or not. He had mastered the art of keeping a perfectly straight face when making a humorous remark. The only way one could detect his real purpose was to spot the twinkle in his eye.

The holiday cruise wound to an end, and the Churchills

flew back to London from the tiny Gibraltar airfield, traveling with holidaymakers in a tourist-class Viscount. Once back in London, one of the first social engagements Sir Winston undertook was a visit to the Connaught Theatre at Worthing to see his daughter Sarah as Rose in Terence Rattigan's play *Variations on a Theme*.

This was only the second time he had seen Sarah act. He sat with his party in the third row and I remember him turning to a man sitting near him and saying, "Don't worry, the cigars will not come out during the performance." He was very proud of Sarah as an actress. Later that year he visited the Scala Theatre to see her as Peter Pan. He was surrounded by his grandchildren that night and undoubtedly enjoyed the Barrie play as much as they did.

Sir Winston could never be described as a great theatre-goer. An evening out for him usually meant attending a dinner, and whenever this happened, Lady Churchill would make up a party with some friends and quietly slip off to a West End show. If they went to the theatre together Sir Winston and Lady Churchill sat in the front stalls, no farther back than the fifth row. This was so that Sir Winston could catch all the dialogue. Another reason was that he had difficulty in climbing stairs and it would have been impracticable for him to sit in the circle. His presence in the stalls always caused a stir in the audience, and the rise of the curtain was occasionally delayed because of the added attraction. He loved sitting with young people, and their comments on the show caused him many a chuckle. During the production of *Peter Pan* one of his grandchildren exclaimed when Sarah made her entrance, "Oh. It's Aunt Sarah!"

At the end of October that year, after spending two weeks at Roquebrune at the Riviera home of Emery Reves, his literary agent, Churchill flew to Paris to receive the Cross of the Liberation from General de Gaulle. The medal consisted of the Cross of Lorraine mounted on a miniature sword and decorated with green and black ribbons. It was rather ironic because during the war Sir Winston had once said, "Of all the crosses I have to bear the heaviest is the Cross of Lorraine." Sir Winston had been proposed for the Cross of the Liberation in 1946, but for some reason the list was closed and he was given the Medaille Militaire instead.

General de Gaulle presented the award under the copper-leaved trees of his garden at the Hotel Matignon, the French Premier's official residence. It was a very emotional moment. Both men stood bareheaded, face-to-face. De Gaulle removed his spectacles and bent down from his great height to kiss Sir Winston on both cheeks. It was their first meeting since the war years.

As the General pinned the Cross of the Liberation on his friend's coat, he said it was for his "decisive contribution to saving the freedom of the world." For Sir Winston, the ceremony was proof that France realized the debt she owed him.

III

Cigars

Sɪʀ Wɪɴꜱᴛᴏɴ nearly always went to bed at about midnight, except when he had guests who liked to sit around the fire late at night drinking brandies and smoking cigars. As I have said, the fires both at Hyde Park Gate and Chartwell were always log fires and, when he was at his London home, a shooting brake used to bring the logs up to town from the country. The gardeners at Chartwell cut the logs, which were always packed in large paper sacks.

Sir Winston always saw his guests safely off to bed before retiring himself; Chartwell was so buried in the country that invariably dinner guests stayed the night. He would go up to his bedroom on the first floor by the automatic elevator specially installed for him on the instructions of Lady Churchill. He always seemed to be smoking a cigar when he went up to bed and even when he undressed for the night he kept it firmly clenched between his teeth. Sometimes it would be out, but on other occasions, when it was glowing, I marveled that he did not set fire to himself. He wore shirts that buttoned down the front but never unbuttoned them, preferring instead to pull them over his head. Bunching shirt and vest together, he used to sweep them over his head without touching the cigar, quite a remarkable feat.

Sir Winston never believed in wearing pajamas in bed, his only concession being to wear his silk vest on very cold nights. I could never understand his wearing the vest because the room temperature was always 70° Fahrenheit and the bedroom windows were never opened. We ventilated the bedroom by opening the bathroom windows to provide for some circulation of air. He hated drafts of any kind, and at Chartwell his bedroom windows were specially sealed up with putty.

I must admit that his habit of sleeping without pajamas caused the staff a few problems. He would throw everyone into a great panic by climbing out of bed unaided first thing in the morning and walking onto the landing, calling for assistance.

I shall never forget one young housemaid on her first day at Hyde Park Gate screaming at the top of her voice when she came face-to-face with him leaning heavily on his stick at the top of the stairs. The bell at his bedside was not working, we discovered later, and he decided to set off on his own. It being an old house, the walls were so thick that no one could hear him calling.

It never occurred to him to put on a dressing gown. Walking about in the nude was something that seemed completely natural to him. He used to put on a bedjacket when he sat up in bed for breakfast, but whenever he rose to take his bath, he would make his way to the bathroom tugging off the jacket as he did so. Fortunately, at both his homes the bathroom led straight off the bedroom, so there was never any danger of his bumping into anything or anyone.

One of my jobs with Sir Winston was to look after his cigars. These were always kept at Chartwell, stored immediately above his bedroom in a tiny room that led off the study. It was filled with Churchilliana: polo sticks, a ceremonial sword, an Arab chieftain's dress, a dozen or so pictures presented at some time or other, numerous cigar boxes, some quite ornate and many carrying inscriptions on special gold and silver plates.

The cigars themselves were laid out on shelves according to size and whether or not they were wrapped. Labels were stuck on the shelves reading "wrapped" and "naked," "large" and "small." When I joined Sir Winston in 1958 there were about three to four thousand cigars in the room. One of the principal suppliers was Simon Camacho, president of the Camacho Cigar Company of Miami, Florida. For more than two years he shipped more than a hundred of his seven-inch handmade "Camacho Churchills" to Sir Winston each month.

The supply dropped off, however, during the Cuban crisis because of the difficulty of obtaining the raw tobacco, a trade embargo having been placed on all American imports from Cuba. Supplies picked up after Camacho managed to get around this difficulty; sometimes he managed to purchase his Cuban tobacco through other sources.

All Sir Winston had to pay was the import duty each time the boxes arrived by mail. The cigars were wrapped in protective cellophane and came in boxes stamped "Handmade Camacho Churchills."

Camacho himself said, "I am pleased and honored that in our small way we are able to provide pleasure for this wonderful man."

Equally appreciated were the slightly shorter Cuban "Romeo y Julieta" cigars.

Cigars were always being sent to him from all over the world. One of the regular suppliers was Erik Stokkebye, of Odense, Denmark, whose "Santa Maria" Havanas always came in aluminum cases carrying the inscriptions "Supplier to the Right Honorable Sir Winston S. Churchill" and "Dedicated to the Rt. Hon. Sir Winston Churchill, Doctor philosophiae honoris causa, The University of Copenhagen, October 10th, 1950."

Mr. Stokkebye sent the smallest cheroots I have ever seen to Lady Churchill at Christmastime and on birthdays. Sir Winston, of course, never smoked these and, indeed, rarely smoked anything other than thick, long Cuban cigars. Occasionally he enjoyed a Jamaican cigar, especially the "Park Lane" ones, but on the whole he was happy with Havanas.

When Sir Winston was eighty-three, he was smoking between seven and eight cigars a day, sometimes more. It all depended on the company and the circumstances. He always believed in smoking them down to the last inch, regarding the last part of the cigar as the best.

If he had two-thirds or even a half of a particularly good cigar still to smoke at bedtime, he would always save it for relighting in the morning. He never believed in stubbing or cutting the cigar end off, preferring to leave it to go out by itself in a deep ashtray.

Sir Winston's favorite ashtray was one given to him by Emery Reves. It was made of silver, pagoda-shaped with a trough on top to hold a cigar. This ashtray was always at Sir Winston's side, used in the drawing and dining rooms but never in the bedroom. It had a matching silver matchbox cover, a present from Sarah. In his bedroom he always used a deep ashtray of Venetian glass.

There was always a certain ritual with the silver ashtray whenever he was away from home. On the Riviera it was ceremoniously handed over to the headwaiter of his private dining room each day before lunch, and then returned with great decorum after dinner. The silver ashtray was always packed in a special suitcase, along with boxes of large matches, small matches, spare packs of playing cards, the green baize cloth for the card games, and "the assortment" box, the special box he had filled with a variety of cigars he had in stock.

Before the Cuban crisis he always smoked the cigars he received from his friend in Havana, the only variation being on birthdays or at Christmastime when he would try out those given him as presents. One night when he and I were alone in the drawing room he asked me if I would like to smoke one of the giant Cuban cigars. I told him that I smoked only cigarettes. Sir Winston chuckled and replied, "Too many of those will kill you."

He spent a lot of money on cigars after his Cuban supply dried up, and it took me a little while to get used to the fact that in two days his cigar consumption was the equivalent of my weekly salary.

Often he would give cigars away to close friends and visiting dignitaries and employees. His detective Murray, his chauffeur Bullock, even his female nurses were all given cigars from time to time. One Australian nurse, Miss Glenda McAlpin, used to sit with him late at night in the drawing room, both smoking cigars. His daughter Mary took after her father, and occasionally I saw her enjoy a cigar after dinner. Lady Churchill always smoked cigarettes and never more than one or two a day.

Sir Winston's suits were constantly going in for repair because of holes caused by cigar burns. He used to burn his suits this way when he became too engrossed in reading; the cigar would droop slightly and catch the lapel.

Despite the experts' view that one should always use a cigar cutter, he always used a match to pierce the end, which he first moistened. He would then take the cigar and blow through it from the other end to clear the passage he had made. He had a special cigar piercer on his watch chain but never used it. Two cigar cutters, one made of gold and ebony, presented to him on special occasions, were similarly ignored. Also, he always used the same kind of matches to light his cigars—special two-inch-long ones flown over from Canada in huge cartons. Whenever Sir Winston was at Chartwell the cigar ends were saved by the staff for one of the gardeners who used to break them up and smoke them in his pipe as he worked in the grounds.

Cigars and brandy go together, and without any doubt at all, fine old champagne brandy was Sir Winston's favorite drink. Whisky was a close second, champagne third. But he loved to drink wine at meals and took it for both lunch and dinner. It was always white wine; he did not hold with the idea of switching to red wine for a meat course. His attitude was one of, "I *like* wine and I intend having it *whatever* I eat." This was typical of the man. He knew what he wanted and most of the time people acceded to his wishes.

For a few months in 1959 I left his service. His health had never been better and it seemed as if there was little I could do.

When I handed in my notice, he seemed amazed that I should want to leave his service. I told him, "You are not sick now, Sir Winston, and I want to pursue my nursing career."

He replied, "But I may be ill tomorrow."

It was obvious to me that he did not relish the prospect of a change.

"Would you return if I sent for you?" he asked me.

I felt very flattered. I told him that I would. It made me feel that my work was fully appreciated.

I was not away long. I returned after receiving a letter from his private secretary asking me if I could return "as soon as possible." It was an irresistible invitation and within a few days I was packing my bags. All my early nervousness had gone, and Sir Winston obviously liked me at his side.

Once more I was constantly at his elbow, making sure

37

he had everything he wanted. Although I was engaged as a nurse, my job had by now grown into something far bigger. I was also the supplier of cigars, the valet, the one who looked after his pets, and a constant buffer between his powerful personality and others.

He was far from helpless at this stage; indeed he shaved himself with an electric razor every morning until his eighty-ninth year. He always shaved at midday before he got up for his bath, plugging the lead into the angle-poised lamp socket at his elbow.

He had two electric razors, one at Chartwell and the other at Hyde Park Gate. In earlier years he used a safety razor but switched because he had only a very light beard and found lathering too much bother. He used a special aftershave lotion, bought from Boots, and preferred the lotion to be mild and nonscented.

He did not like his toilet requisites to be perfumed in any way. He used a very expensive soap, always the same yellow bars, which were ordered by Lady Churchill's secretary. He was most fastidious about his teeth, brushing them three times a day and taking a good fifteen minutes over each brushing. Instead of toothpaste he used a white powder preparation kept in a glass bowl. He had six toothbrushes, three yellow and three green, and used a different one each time. The toothbrushes were laid out in a line and whenever he had finished cleaning his teeth he would put the brush he had used at the end of the row. Every three months he paid a visit to the dentist at his office just off Harley Street. Most of his teeth were his own and the constant attention he paid them ensured that he never had any trouble.

Everything in his bedroom was regimented. He had a pair of hairbrushes at the side of his bed that he used before retiring for the night and again first thing in the morning. He would hold a brush in each hand and carefully use them to stroke his hair straight back over his head. Six strokes every time. He even brushed the parts where there was no hair. He had a second set of hairbrushes, bone with silver monograms "W.S.C." and used these after applying hair lotion before going down for lunch or dinner. His hair was cut once a month in his bedroom. A chair was set at his dressing table and a dust sheet laid out on the floor. The hairdresser was always nervous, especially when Sir Winston, who obviously considered the whole thing a waste of time, growled, "That's enough, leave it alone." The hairdresser never trimmed his eyebrows, which were always brushed upward.

He wore two shirts a day. Usually it was a cream one in the morning and a white one in the evening, when he either changed into a dinner jacket or slipped on a maroon zip-suit, which he wore with a black bow tie. He used ready-made bow ties in the last few years of his life because they were easier to manage. There were three different kinds in his dressing-table drawer: two black ones for evening wear, two black polka-dot ties for whenever he went to the House of Commons, and two blue polka-dot ties to go with his lounge suits. He had about six ordinary ties but rarely used them. One of these was his Churchill College tie, another was a plum red one bought in the south of France.

He liked anything that saved time. Even his shoes had zip-fasteners. Only one pair laced up and these were the patent-leather evening shoes worn when he went out for dinner. At home he liked to wear slippers. He had three pairs: one in black leather, one in red velvet with his monogram on the toecap, and another in blue velvet, also monogrammed.

He was a tidy man who liked things around him to be organized. Everything had to be in its right place and he would be quite upset if things were moved. Routine was everything to him, no matter where he was. Every night he had a cup of cold consommé on retiring, even if he had just returned from a big banquet. This was just one of the many little things that had to fit into place throughout the day.

He was an intensely practical person. He built the fish-ponds and the swimming pool at Chartwell when he was "in the wilderness" politically. He had bought Chartwell with the money he earned from *The World Crisis,* his survey of World War One. During the last years, when he was unable to do manual jobs, he still went round the gardens making suggestions; things like having the fish-ponds drained, cleaned and refilled, and having the small lake wired round and a flickering light fitted to prevent the foxes getting at the black swans.

The autumn of 1959 saw the unveiling of what I believe to be the only full-length statue of Sir Winston in the country. It was the work of the Scottish sculptor David McFall, and it certainly proved controversial.

It was erected in Sir Winston's constituency, Woodford, Essex, a standing figure nine feet high and cast in bronze. The great man did not see it until it was unveiled by Lord Montgomery, and, although he complimented the sculptor, I believe that he was not extremely impressed.

Mr. McFall was commissioned for the work by local people, but as soon as they saw the preliminary study they objected on the grounds that it made Sir Winston look too old. They felt the monument should show him at the height of his power and that it should look more like the Churchill of the war years.

A lot of people disagreed with them, but Mr. McFall submitted a new head, which the locals felt was much better. But when photographs of the new work appeared in the newspapers, the controversy flared up again; some thought the sculptor had missed the essential cherubic aspect of Sir Winston's face and that the work was too wooden.

Nevertheless a large crowd turned out for the unveiling ceremony, and, with a local territorial unit acting as guard of honor, Lord Montgomery pulled the cord. From the set of the shoulders, the angle of the head, and the jut of the chin, the statue was instantly recognizable. The full-length figure in a lounge suit was in typical Churchillian pose: left hand pulling back the flap of the jacket as if reaching for his watch. There were, however, quite a few quizzical looks from the crowd.

Sir Winston, wearing a black homburg, black overcoat, and white muffler, kept glancing up at the statue during the ceremony as if he were not too sure about it. He admitted in a short speech that it was always difficult to comment on a work portraying oneself.

That Christmas a rather unusual thing happened. Sir Winston was presented with a gold keyless pocket watch by an admirer, Mr. Morris Benjamin, a chartered surveyor living in Eaton Square. Sir Winston recognized it immediately; it was his own watch. This, briefly, was the watch's story. His father, Lord Randolph Churchill, gave the watch to his son in 1893. The date was inscribed inside. Five years later Sir Winston presented the watch to his faithful aide, Thomas Walden, who later died.

Walden's widow had the watch put up for sale at Christie's, and it was bought for £420 by Mr. Benjamin. Not long afterward Mr. Benjamin called at Hyde Park Gate and gave the watch back to Sir Winston, who was surprised and delighted at seeing it again.

At that time Sir Winston went as usual to a Christmas pantomime with all his grandchildren. It was invariably a very jolly occasion, with the excited children calling at the London home for lunch before moving off in a fleet of cars to the theatre. Among the party in orchestra stalls were his chauffeur, Mr. Joe Bullock, and his wife and his detective, Sergeant Edmund Murray, and his wife.

Murray, who replaced Inspector Walter Thompson, Sir Winston's bodyguard during the war years, was an ex-French Foreign Legionnaire and always carried a small pistol in a shoulder holster under his left armpit. He was a good, efficient bodyguard, blunt, broad-shouldered, and the perfect man for dealing with people who pushed forward to be seen with his charge. He always announced himself as, "Sergeant Edmund Murray of Scotland Yard," and Sir Winston had no bigger admirer. Like his master, he painted in oils, and whenever Sir Winston was about to set off on a painting expedition, Murray would check through his oils and brushes, clean his palette, and make sure he had sufficient canvases.

Sir Winston had a great affection for him and never allowed anyone to criticize him or interfere with his duties. Murray in return was a loyal servant who did a good job under difficult circumstances. He often had to be extremely diplomatic in handling people, especially when we were abroad. One must remember that everywhere Sir Winston went crowds gathered, even in the Casino at Monte Carlo when he was playing Trente et Quarante, or when on some minor expedition.

Murray had a thankless job. At times when we were at Chartwell it must have been unspeakably boring for him to be hanging around, particularly in the later years when Sir Winston did less traveling. Murray had to be there every day working from 9 A.M. until 5 P.M. He rarely, if ever, worked weekends, and it was a joke among the staff that would-be assassins were warned off then. He always went with Sir Winston to the Commons, and on their return he would be invited into the drawing room for a whisky and soda and a cigar. There never seemed to be any danger of anyone assassinating Sir Winston in the later years, but Murray always had to be on his guard against cranks and crackpots. In practically every newspaper picture of Sir Winston one can find Murray's bulky figure either helping Sir Winston or just standing at his elbow. He would never put a foot out of line when on duty, but in off-duty moments he used to discuss painting at great length with Sir Winston, often picking up tips on technique. Whenever visitors to Chartwell were shown over Sir Winston's garden studio, Murray acted as unofficial guide, being particularly well informed about each painting hanging on the walls.

IV

An Octogenarian in High Seas

SIR WINSTON spent many of his holidays on board
Onassis' yacht *Christina* but one of the most enjoyable was
the three-week cruise in the Caribbean early in 1960. We
set off from London Airport in a BEA Viscount, and the
plan was that we should land at Gibraltar where a reception committee was waiting to greet Sir Winston before
he boarded the yacht. It did not quite work out that way.

The whole journey was packed with drama. To start
with, when we arrived at London Airport Sir Winston saw
a plane do a pancake landing right in front of him and his
departure had to be delayed until the runway was cleared.
Then, when we were over Gibraltar, the aircraft ran into
gale-force winds. I remember us dropping like a stone and
all the luggage tumbling out of the overhead racks. Jane
Montague Browne, the six-year-old daughter of Sir Winston's secretary, was with the party and screamed when she
was hurled against a table, hitting her head.

Jane and two other children were crying and quite a few
of us were scared by the buffeting the plane was receiving.
But the calmest man on board was Sir Winston, who
quietly puffed away at his seven-inch-long cigar, gazing out

of the window as if nothing was wrong. Technically, of course, he should have put the cigar out, as the plane was about to land, but he chose to ignore the rules. We did not like to tell him to put his cigar out, relying on the stewardess to do our dirty work for us. It took a great deal of persuasion to make Sir Winston part with his cigar, but when a pretty air hostess quietly made the point he usually gave in.

As we came in at Gibraltar, the pilot overshot the runway and our aircraft roared out across the sea; landing was a tricky operation in certain conditions. He tried a second approach and overshot again. Deciding against a third try, he headed for Tangier Airport, just across the Straits, a diversion that meant we had to spend the night there.

We landed in a high wind and were driven straight to the Consulate where drinks were served while rooms were hurriedly prepared at a hotel. Sir Winston, I remember, refused to go down to dinner wearing a lounge suit, and there was a delay while a search was made for his dinner jacket, carefully packed away in one of the sixteen almost identical suitcases. After the meal the hotel guests stood and applauded as Sir Winston left the dining room, while the orchestra played "For He's a Jolly Good Fellow." He retired early and had a good night's sleep before leaving early next morning to join Onassis' yacht, which had come across from Gibraltar overnight.

During the cruise everyone on board was seasick except Sir Winston, who stayed in the salon champing on his cigar, chewing as usual at its end. Lady Churchill was slightly seasick and remained in her cabin.

The first two days of the cruise were very rough, and although the yacht had stabilizers that were supposed to reduce the roll by ninety percent, I hate to think what it would have been like had these not been fitted. The days drifted by, Sir Winston spending most of his time sitting on deck watching the dolphins and flying fish, playing bezique with the other guests and, after dinner, watching films. When we reached the West Indies, we spent two weeks lazily touring round the islands. Throughout the whole cruise he and Onassis hit it off perfectly. I am sure Onassis did not play host to Sir Winston for any ulterior motive. He was genuinely fond of him, striking a delicate balance in their relations which never at any time showed any signs of subservience on his part. He always rose to the occasion whenever his guest was in a difficult mood, knowing exactly how to handle him. He was a good host and nothing was too much trouble. Everything necessary for Sir Winston's comfort was always laid on for each occasion, right down to the times Sir Winston used to go ashore accompanied by a special picnic basket containing whisky, soda and ice.

Onassis was always most anxious to see that Sir Winston ate and drank exactly what he wanted, even to the extent of slipping him a couple of spoonfuls of caviar when the ladies had gone to the dining room after cocktails on the poop deck. Sir Winston, on a restricted diet to stabilize his weight, was forbidden by his doctors to have more than one portion of caviar because of the fat content.

The cruise round the Caribbean islands was a constant worry to those looking after him. Being responsible for an octogenarian moving around a yacht that was frequently in high seas was somewhat daunting, especially when one had difficulty keeping one's own feet.

One of the guests on the yacht was Lord Moran, Sir Winston's personal physician. He was an old friend, and although frail-looking, was an extremely active Yorkshire-born doctor with a gentle voice and scholarly manner. He was the man of whom Sir Winston once said: "To his unfailing care I probably owe my life."

Lord Moran had a slight stoop and gray, thinning hair.

I remember that whenever he called on his patient he invariably said, "I will just warm my hands," before carrying out his examination.

He was on board for one main reason. The yacht had to cross the Atlantic, and there was no chance of getting medical help for about ten days should anything have gone wrong. When, later on, Sir Winston visited the Greek islands, the situation was different because his doctor in the south of France, Dr. David Roberts, could have been flown out from Monte Carlo and have been at his side within an hour.

As usual, Sir Winston, then eighty-five, wanted to inspect the most inaccessible parts of the yacht. A visit to the bridge, for example, meant he had to climb a number of near-vertical stairways. It was a feat in itself to get him on and off the yacht. One was terrified of a sudden lurch of the gangplank. The yacht was always anchored off-shore to maintain privacy for Sir Winston, as wherever he went, hundreds of sightseers filled the quayside and scores of small boats came out for a short-range inspection through binoculars. Being anchored in the harbor meant that whenever he went ashore he had to negotiate the crossover from yacht to launch and then from launch to quayside, a double hazard. Fortunately the crew was impeccably trained and there was never a mishap.

The cruise was enlivened by noisy music from the West Indian steel bands. I can describe the sound of these only as being similar to having four stereo record players going at the same time in each corner of a room. They were deafening.

Two of the best steel bands in the Caribbean played specially for Sir Winston. They were the "Hell's Gate" band, which performed on board the yacht and made the knives and forks bounce off the tables, and the "Brute Force" band, which played at a reception ashore. Whenever I think of that Caribbean cruise my most vivid recollection is of the completely abandoned playing of the bands and the infectious happy-go-lucky attitude the people had to life.

The reception Sir Winston received when he arrived at Bridgetown, Barbados, was unbelievable. Hours before the *Christina's* launch chugged across to the shore, hundreds of small boats had massed round the quayside approaches. So many people shinned up the masts of the moored schooners that I thought some boats were in danger of sinking, they were so overloaded.

There was a great roar of welcome when he stepped ashore, and the police band struck up. Sir Winston, I remember, kept his yachting cap on for the inspection of the guard of honor but switched headgear as soon as he climbed into a waiting open car. He loved different hats, and this time he chose a white Stetson that matched his white tropical suit. He waved it as he drove off to have lunch eight miles away with his host, Mr. Ronald Tree, an old friend.

Mr. Tree, a former Conservative M.P., was a wartime colleague of Sir Winston.

Onassis suffered one big disappointment on the cruise. He had hoped to sail along the Florida coastline, one of the most attractive in the world. But with the delay at Tangier and the rough crossing, the trip took longer than had been expected. So, instead of sailing up to New York as planned, he sailed to Puerto Rico and the Churchills flew home via the Azores.

Sir Winston had to be back in London for the first week of April when General de Gaulle was paying a state visit. I remember the occasion well. They met in Westminster Hall surrounded by dazzling pageantry. De Gaulle was addressing members of both Houses, and his speech, full of ringing phrases and stirring gestures, recalled the war years. He hinted, amid laughter, that Sir Winston and he had not always seen eye to eye on certain points. It was a very dramatic occasion, with de Gaulle's speech being cheered and applauded for well over a minute.

The day before, however, there had been another dramatic moment that never leaked out. It happened at Hyde Park Gate when the General decided to make an unscheduled visit. I was running the water for Sir Winston's bath and was rather keyed up. The whole house was bustling with activity in preparation for the General's visit.

Sir Winston was resting in bed and called me out of the bathroom to fetch something. I went into his bedroom and completely forgot about the running bath taps. It was only when I saw water flooding from the bathroom that I realized I had not turned off the taps.

The overflow hole on the bath had been specially sealed up because Sir Winston liked his bath full right to the brim. The bath was normally two-thirds filled, and when Sir Winston got in, the water then rose to lap the top.

The bathroom was completely awash. Slowly it dawned on me where the water was going. It was cascading through the ceiling into the room in which General de Gaulle was to be received.

The situation was nightmarish. I felt as though Hyde Park Gate was the one place on earth I would like to escape from. I wanted to quietly slip away somewhere. But there was only one thing to do: brave it out. So I made my way downstairs, at each step feeling more and more depressed. When I got to the drawing room I found the situation was worse than I had imagined.

To my horror I saw that the torrent had split the entire drawing-room ceiling. The water was pouring through straight onto an antique chair and bouncing off onto the expensive carpet. Lady Churchill came in and was in a highly agitated state. Looking up at the cracked ceiling, she said anxiously, "What on earth will we do if the ceiling falls in when General de Gaulle is here?"

An army of workers was hurriedly assembled. Collecting every available mop, bucket, and spare cloth in the house, they carried out the salvage operation at top speed. Amazingly enough, Sir Winston knew nothing of what had happened. He was upstairs in bed, still reading, probably wondering why his bath was taking such a time to prepare.

By the time the General arrived, the damage had been neatly camouflaged and the only clue to what had happened was the ceiling marked with a great dark patch. De Gaulle was so engrossed in meeting Sir Winston that he did not notice the ominous crack above his head and the visit passed off perfectly well.

At that time Sir Winston was wearing a small hearing aid in his right ear, with the switch under the ear lobe. This led many people to believe he was very deaf, but it was not the case. He had the impish habit of flicking the switch to "off" whenever a conversation bored him, continuing to nod from time to time, giving the impression that he was in deep thought.

It was a typical Churchillian ruse and one could only admire the way he disguised the maneuver. Sometimes he would pretend he was scratching the back of his ear absent-mindedly; at other times he would achieve the switch-off by thoughtfully stroking the side of his neck. Every morning I had the job of fitting the hearing aid into his right ear and naturally always set the thing at "on." But frequently Lady Churchill would call in, perhaps feeling that her husband was out of touch with the conversation, and ask me to adjust the volume on Sir Winston's instrument. I always found that the hearing aid had been switched right off.

V

"You were very rude to me, you know!"

IT is generally agreed that Sir Winston excelled when it came to painting in oils. Had he done nothing else but paint in his lifetime, the experts say, he could have been a great artist. His brick studio near the stables at Chartwell was always stacked with his paintings, the value of which must have run into a very great sum. I remember the hordes of sightseers making a beeline for the studio each time the gardens were opened to the public, usually in May. They would queue up to stand on tiptoe and peer through the studio windows, excitedly pointing out the pictures to one another. Over four hundred canvases were stored in the studio at Chartwell at one time, and I was told the estimated value was "at least £3,000 each." They may well be worth ten times that sum in years to come.

On one rare occasion one of Sir Winston's paintings was put up for auction. It was his "Cork Trees at Mimizan," which he had painted in 1924 when he was staying in the south of France with the Duke of Westminster. Sir Winston gave it to help the World Refugee Fund, and it was put up for auction at Sotheby's in the spring of 1960. The sale rooms were packed on the night of the auction and there was a gasp from the audience when it was sold to an American for £7,400.

It was the first picture Sir Winston had ever submitted for a public auction, and Lady Churchill, elegant in a lilac dress with two strings of pearls, was there to see the painting fetch what at that time was the highest price earned by a living English artist. Sir Winston was at home, and the minute the picture was sold, Lady Churchill asked a friend: "Ring Sir Winston at once and let him know."

Whenever Sir Winston expressed a desire to paint, Murray, his detective, would lay out the tubes of oil colors on a collapsible table, and then set up the easel and erect his chair. Always Murray would gently squeeze a little of each of the primary colors onto Sir Winston's mixing board; he never used a palette in later years.

The mixing board was attached to the easel sticking out at right angles. This was sometimes rather a nuisance because Sir Winston would become engrossed in his painting, lean forward to add a delicate detail, and drag his sleeve across the board. He ruined at least two gray suits in this way. He had a white smock but frequently would attack the canvas before we had time to get him into it.

He never worried about getting paint onto his clothes; Lady Churchill, ever anxious, would be the one who worried. Her husband often greeted guests for lunch or tea wearing a paint-smeared jacket. "It's not really noticeable," he would say whenever anyone tried to persuade him to change.

Sir Winston was not a great collector of paintings. Those that hung in his London and country homes were portraits of his ancestors, portraits of himself, or his own paintings, which easily outnumbered the others.

In 1960 Sir Winston took two cruises on the yacht *Christina:* one to the Caribbean and the other around the Greek islands. For the second cruise Onassis had twelve guests on board when he picked up Sir Winston and Lady Churchill in Venice after they had flown out from London Airport. Greeted by crowds everywhere, they did a grand tour of Venice's Grand Canal in a motorboat before joining the yacht, which was lying off St. Mark's square.

Dame Margot Fonteyn and her husband Dr. Roberto Arias were among the guests and spent a lot of time chattering with Sir Winston on the poop deck as the yacht cruised through the peaceful waters of the Mediterranean.

The ballerina has a wonderful personality and a gentle and sweet nature that made her an immediate favorite with Sir Winston. She is devoted to her husband, who is rather quiet and studious, not at all like the excitable hand-waving characters one usually expects from his part of the world. Dame Margot and her husband were among the most popular of all the guests on the yacht.

But the big moment of the cruise round the islands was Sir Winston's meeting with President Tito of Yugoslavia. This took place at Split.

Sir Winston went ashore with Onassis, Lady Churchill, and the secretary. The four met Tito privately and took refreshments with him. The next morning a Yugoslavian Navy motorboat brought Tito out to the yacht for lunch. The yacht's three stewards, wearing white jackets and white gloves, served the meal at the long table on deck and afterward Sir Winston and Tito decided to pose together for photographs taken by the guests and crew. There was never any question of press photographers taking pictures on board the yacht.

I remember thinking how different the two men looked. Tito, broad-shouldered, tanned and rugged, looked very impressive. Sir Winston, slightly shorter and, in comparison, frail, looked pale beside Tito's tan. Sir Winston's skin did not sunburn and always seemed to keep the same pinkness. Tito spoke English and the two great leaders found lots to talk about before they eventually shook hands and Tito left in his launch.

Onassis took great care to ensure that Madame Tito, who accompanied her husband, was not left out of things, and I remember seeing Lady Churchill deep in conversation with her. When the yacht reached Crete, Margot Fonteyn had to leave the cruise. She flew back to London to sit on the selection committee of the Royal Academy of Dancing, obviously regarding this as an important duty that had precedence over her holiday.

Crete was a tranquil island, beautifully isolated in the deep-blue Mediterranean. Sir Winston must have thought of the grim battle fought on the island when the German paratroops invaded in 1941 and the British and Commonwealth defenders put up such a gallant fight against hopeless odds. He went ashore and toured the island by car, returning to the yacht for lunch. At about five o'clock on the first evening a group of Cretan dancers, wearing their national costume, came on board and gave a display on the poop deck. Later a special dinner party was given for Sir Winston at Canea on Crete by the Liberal leader Sophocles Venizelos. Throughout the whole evening Sir Winston impassively enjoyed himself, carrying out conversations through an interpreter. Onassis enjoyed such dinners, and they helped to vary the holiday, much of which was spent on board. The following day when we reached Heraklion, Sir Winston left the yacht for a short car trip to see the ruins of King Minos's palace at Knossos. He was back for dinner and the usual film show that he always enjoyed so keenly.

Then the *Christina* sailed on to Corinth, where Onassis and his party went ashore to see the ruins. Onassis and Sir Winston always had the same outlook when it came to holidays: to relax and thoroughly enjoy whatever they felt like doing.

It was a rather warm day when the party landed at Corinth, and the two friends obviously were not in a mood to go trekking round ruins. They said they would stay on the beach while Lady Churchill, Mr. and Mrs. Montague Browne, and I went off sightseeing. When we returned some time later there was no sign of Sir Winston or Onassis.

We eventually found them in a humble bar just off the beach. They were sitting there drinking whiskies and eating fried fish out of a communal bowl. The proprietor, beaming all over his face, was obviously thrilled at having such important clientele. No wonder he was rubbing his hands; his bar had suddenly attained a new status. Lady Churchill, I thought, might have been annoyed, but she was not. She smiled and said, "How amusing!"

The cruise ended in Athens, where Onassis drove the Churchills to the airport and saw them off on a Comet, one of the Olympic Airways fleet, which he owned.

Two months later they spent their fifty-second wedding anniversary at Chartwell. It was a quiet family affair and not at all like September 12th, 1908, when cordons of police held back the crowds for their wedding at St. Margaret's, Westminster. Later in 1960 Sir Winston and Lady Churchill flew back to the south of France to spend a month at the Hotel de Paris in Monte Carlo. The holiday was as informal as ever. Even General de Gaulle dropped in. He was touring the Riviera making speeches about the Algerian situation and interrupted his tour to meet Sir Winston in the library of the Nice police station. They chatted together for half an hour before the General continued his tour and Sir Winston went back to his holiday.

He had a suite on the eighth floor of the Hotel de Paris overlooking the harbor and the Palace. Naturally his arrival at the hotel was quite an event, and the foyer always seemed to be filled with people with whom he had to shake hands before he could go up to his room. There was invariably much bowing and bobbing.

His room was stacked with flowers whenever he arrived, each bouquet wrapped in cellophane and decorated with pink ribbon and a large card. The management made sure he had a large bed, which was normally against a wall. However, it was pushed round the room on occasions; let me explain.

The view from the French windows of the suite was breathtaking, and because Sir Winston did not want to miss it when he awoke each morning, he would ask me to push the bed across the room to the windows. This was not as easy as it sounds. The bed was a heavy ornate thing and heavier for Sir Winston being in it.

After much huffing and puffing I would get the bed up against the windows. As I straightened up and regained my breath, Sir Winston would say, "Not quite right." I would say, "Which way?" And he would reply, "A little to left . . . back a little. That will do."

I would then leave the room. Almost immediately he would call me back into the room. "I think it should go a little more this way," he would say, indicating the direction with a sweep of his hand.

This routine took place nearly every morning. It all seems rather amusing now, but in all fairness, it was a superb view. It was well worth moving the bed.

Once he was installed in the hotel, Sir Winston always entered and left by the rear entrance. This was because there were too many stairs at the front: a flight up from street level and then two more flights after the foyer-lounge. At the rear it was much easier: just two flights, one a mere six steps and the other adapted for a ramp to take a wheel chair.

A crowd of photographers always gathered on the sidewalk whenever Sir Winston left the hotel, and they attracted sightseers until the entrance was a solid mass of people, all patiently waiting for the hotel's most celebrated guest. When he did leave, it was usually for an automobile ride, accompanied by his secretary, a member of the family, and a nurse. The car was followed by another one driven by a French detective with Murray at his side. They in turn were followed by a line of press cars until there was quite a procession going through the town.

During the summer of 1960, Prince Rainier and Princess Grace of Monaco visited Sir Winston at his hotel and had lunch with him in his suite. I remember them arriving and Sir Winston rising to his feet to bow.

Afterward they all sat out on the terrace until mid-afternoon. Sir Winston was very impressed with Princess Grace's beauty and charm and got on very well with her husband. That evening they entertained him for dinner at the Palace and put on a special film for him.

Other luncheon guests at the Hotel de Paris were Somerset Maugham, the author, and his secretary, Alan Searle. Maugham's villa was just along the coast.

The famous author looked very much as I had imagined: rather fragile and with heavily lined skin that appeared almost transparent. His voice was quite soft and gentle and, knowing that Sir Winston was slightly deaf, he raised it a tone when speaking to him. The two men seemed to have a quiet understanding quite common to elderly people, sitting together and not saying very much, yet content to be in each other's company.

The conversations between them were never very remarkable. As the two sat on the terrace of Sir Winston's apartment at the hotel, the conversation would go something like this:

Somerset Maugham: "Will you paint this visit?"

Sir Winston: "I thought I might do something. I am not sure yet."

Somerset Maugham: "You are very well situated here on the terrace. The view is magnificent."

Sir Winston: "I think it is a splendid view."

The latter remark was typical of Sir Winston. He would never go into raptures over a thing; he would study it, then give a considered opinion.

His guest never stayed too long, probably feeling, like his host, that luncheon parties should not be too protracted after one's eightieth birthday.

Alan Searle, dark-haired and tallish, looked quite young beside Maugham, always being very conservatively dressed, polite and tactful, never intruding in any way when he called at the hotel.

Onassis often called for meals if he was in Monte Carlo, sometimes inviting Sir Winston down to the harbor for lunch on board his yacht.

When he drove through the town, Sir Winston wore his Stetson, but as soon as he went on board the *Christina* he switched to a naval cap. On cruises he would wear this and a blue yachting jacket with brass buttons and white flannels. Even when there was no question of a cruise, the oufit had to be there, just in case.

On days when Sir Winston decided to drive over to Lord Beaverbrook's villa, I always had to take along a bottle of whisky and some soda water. The housekeeper at the villa provided a glass and the ice.

This, of course, was when Lord Beaverbrook was away. He was not always in the south of France when Sir Winston was there but nevertheless threw his villa open to his old friend whenever he cared to drive over. The whisky and soda water went along because if Sir Winston asked for something, no matter where we were at the time, he would expect it to be available.

He spent considerable time that summer at the gaming tables of the Casino. At the time a film company was shooting scenes round the Casino entrance, so he dodged the crowds by going straight through the underground passage that connects it to the Hotel de Paris. While he was playing, Lady Churchill would take shopping strolls along Monte Carlo's Bond-street, the winding half-mile-long Boulevard des Moulins. She occasionally took afternoon tea at the Hotel Metropole.

After a successful visit to the Casino, Sir Winston would return to his hotel happily humming to himself. If, however, he lost, he would be gruff and altogether in a bad humor. He never gambled with large sums of money, and the most he would lose at a sitting would be £50 to £100, quite small beer by Casino standards. The highest amount I remember him winning was £100 playing Trente et Quarante.

The Casino opens at 10 A.M. and remains open all day, sometimes closing at 2 A.M., 3 A.M., or even later, depending on the numbers playing. Sir Winston would go straight to the tables where a place was usually reserved for him. Occasionally, when there was no room, one of the players was asked if he would mind giving up his seat. This did not happen very often because most of the visits to the Casino were in the afternoon when it was not so crowded. I remember him paying only two evening visits.

He bought his chips from the croupier and cashed them himself at the cashier's desk on leaving. His most frequent companion at the tables was, of course, Onassis, although sometimes Mr. Montague Browne went along with him. Murray, the detective, was always in attendance.

My most vivid memory of Sir Winston at the Casino is of his back view as he sat at the tables with a whisky at his elbow, quite oblivious of the stares of the other players and those who wandered across from other tables. He would remain there for an hour or two, surrounded by the horde of onlookers and players continually making rapid calculations on small pads before placing their bets. Some of them bet huge amounts on colors only; it seemed as if everyone had his own system for winning. I was always intrigued by the number of rich elderly women, their fingers covered with rings, who were at the tables day after day, gambling only in very small sums.

When he was not at the gaming tables, Sir Winston was painting. He drove out most days into the mountains behind the town. There he would set up his easel and paint quite happily all alone.

Some days Sir Winston and Lady Churchill drove together from their hotel to Mont Agel, the driver taking him to sit and admire the view and his wife to take morning golf lessons at the Mont Agel Golf Club. Lady Churchill was seventy-four at the time but she obviously felt that her game needed a refresher course! The car would return at teatime to pick them up, slowly driving back into Monte Carlo for the evening.

In the late autumn of 1960 Sir Winston returned to England. It was only a few weeks later that he had a serious fall. He had been out to dinner with Lady Churchill on the night of November 15th, returning to Hyde Park Gate about midnight. Before retiring, he went into her room to say goodnight, leaving me outside the bedroom door.

I heard a thud and Lady Churchill called out: "Howells, come quickly!" I ran in and found Sir Winston lying near the wardrobe in Lady Churchill's dressing room, which lead off the bedroom.

Apparently, having kissed his wife goodnight, he had half-turned to tell her something as he was going out of the door, somehow lost his balance and had fallen against the side of the wardrobe. The corner caught him right between the shoulder blades, fracturing his spine.

He lay on the carpet obviously in great pain. I made him comfortable and phoned Lord Moran, his physician. While he was on his way I checked to make sure no limb was broken, then fetched the policeman on duty outside the house to help roll Sir Winston onto a rug. Using this as an improvised stretcher, we carried him to the bed. The policeman was called in because at that time there was no butler in the household and the only other person in the house was Lady Churchill's maid.

Lord Moran arrived and put Sir Winston under light sedation. He spent a fitful night, with Lord Moran sleeping in the room above. Sir Winston was in such pain that his physician could not carry out a proper examination until the next morning. At that time Sir Winston relied heavily on a walking stick following the after-effects of a stroke in 1953.

His right leg dragged slightly and he had a habit of pivoting on his left foot, which meant he sometimes was caught off balance. This caused a great deal of alarm among those around him. Sometimes he would pivot and only just retain his balance. He was warned on many occasions that this was an unwise thing to do, but with usual Churchillian pugnacity he paid little attention to medical advice.

The next day there was an improvement in his condition, and he was taken on a stretcher by ambulance to St. Mary's Hospital, Paddington, for an X-ray. The fracture was confirmed and, although we did not realize it at the time, our troubles were only beginning. Lord Moran asked the hospital to lend Sir Winston a special adjustable bed, which was installed in his bedroom. It was higher and narrower than his own bed, and Sir Winston did not take kindly to it at all, grumbling incessantly about the discomfort it caused.

After a day's battle it was agreed that he could have his own bed back as long as he had fracture boards under the mattress to support his back while he was lying flat and a wooden support at a 45-degree angle to prop him up during the day. He agreed to all this, and it was generally thought to be a good compromise and that he would settle down to the business of getting well again. He had other ideas, however. The next day he announced that he did not intend using the back support and that he was going to take a bath.

Lord Moran called in two other specialists, who advised that Sir Winston should continue to use the wooden supports. Sir Winston was told, but made no comment.

The doctors departed and left the staff to cope as best they could. From that time on it was open warfare between Sir Winston and the nursing team. Every morning there was a struggle to get the angled wooden support into his bed. He firmly resisted all attempts to do this, but it was always installed after a rather exhausting struggle.

On one occasion I remember we had a blazing row over the bedrest and I am afraid we swore at each other. Afterward we made it up. Sir Winston, his bottom lip jutting, said, "You were very rude to me, you know." I told him, "Yes, but you were rude too." Then, with just a hint of a smile, he looked up and said blandly, "Yes, but I *am* a great man." There was no answer to that. He knew, as I and the rest of the world knew, that he was right.

The surprising thing about his fall was that within three weeks all the wooden boards were out of his bed and he was up and about again. It was an extraordinary performance for a man of his age. The doctors all expected him to have great difficulty in walking after this accident.

Six weeks after the fall he drove down to Chartwell for a quiet Christmas with his family. Just before he set off, two men arrived with four green steel boxes. They contained the first four reels of "The Valiant Years," the 26-part film made by the American Broadcasting Company and based on Sir Winston's World War II memoirs. The reels, a gift from the company, were specially "tailored" to fit the projector at Chartwell's basement cinema. The series gave him hours of pleasure.

VI

"Is there a film this evening?"

SIR WINSTON had a passion for the cinema. All his life he had thrived on adventure and, when he could no longer seek it, he had it brought into his own home through films. Chartwell's basement, formerly a dining room, was specially fitted out with two projectors, a cinemascope-size screen, and stereophonic speakers. Sir Winston had a huge chintz-covered armchair to the left of the center aisle about halfway down the long room. On his immediate left was another armchair, usually occupied by his principal guest, and on the other side of the gangway was a six-seater settee where Lady Churchill would sit with the other guests. Behind this luxury row were four rows of hard chairs, filled at every weekend showing by housemaids, butler, cook, gardeners and their wives, secretaries, and car drivers.

The projectionist was a Mr. Shaw, whose wife helped him in the projection box. Sir Winston once introduced him to one of his VIP weekend guests thus: "This is Mr. Shaw, who is our projectionist. He's a Labor man but quite a nice fellow." The films were sent down by rail from London, and whenever Sir Winston was at Chartwell he saw at least three a week.

The film show always started after he had dinner, usually at about 9:15 P.M. Two of the secretaries on the staff would suggest suitable films and check with the film distributors to find out if they were available. The secretaries would then type out a short synopsis of each film and Sir Winston would pick out the ones he wanted to see. His tastes were very wide but he had a special liking for westerns. He saw Alan Ladd in "Shane" several times. We saw John Wayne westerns, Kirk Douglas westerns, Gary Cooper westerns, James Stewart westerns, any western just as long as there was lots of horse riding and gunfighting in it. He also liked period films, ones with lots of dueling and people falling off battlements into moats. All the great epics that ever came out of Hollywood, we had them all. Among his firm favorites were films that featured Steve Reeves as Hercules and Victor Mature as Samson.

Sir Winston loved the costumes and style of period films, especially "The Importance of Being Earnest" and the musical "Gigi," with Leslie Caron and Maurice Chevalier. He had all the Walt Disney films shown and liked "The Living Desert" and "The Incredible Journey." War films were his special favorites: "Bridge on the River Kwai," "All Quiet on the Western Front," "A Time to Love and a Time to Die," "The Longest Day," and "Guns of Navarone."

He had favorite screen stars, usually women: Garbo, Dietrich, and Bergman. "Witness for the Prosecution" with Dietrich was often shown. It had Charles Laughton as well, and he was one of Sir Winston's favorite actors.

"The Valiant Years," in 26 parts, was shown in four special sittings. I spent many hours sitting behind him in the basement cinema watching this series, supplying him with cigars and lighting them. Then, perhaps more than at any other time, I was really conscious of his greatness as I saw film flashbacks of him at his peak and heard his deep voice rasping out his wonderful wartime speeches.

Sometimes, as a supporting program, a special film would be shown of Sir Winston down by the fishponds feeding a little red robin. This robin appeared every time he went down to feed the fish, and Sir Winston was so fond of it that he had the film made. It lasted about a quarter of an hour and was invariably shown when any special guest was down. It always came on to round off the evening after the main feature.

Before dinner Sir Winston would ask me: "Is there a film this evening?" He always relished the thought of going down to the cinema after his meal, and of course his brandy, cigars, special ashtray, and matches would go with him. He liked to share his love of the cinema and would ask members of the staff if they were going to watch the evening's show. When they said they were, he would beam with pleasure and nod his head. He liked to have the household staff around him in the cinema.

One of the problems of these basement film shows at Chartwell, however, was that frequently they were delayed because Sir Winston stayed in the dining room lingering over his brandy and coffee. Many times Lady Churchill had to remind him to join the waiting audience and occasionally the film had to start without his being there. When he eventually *did* arrive, the basement lights were turned up, he was maneuvered into his armchair, and the lights would go down for the film to continue. Throughout the film, the smoke from Sir Winston's cigar used to curl up through the beam from the projection box. When the show was over, the guests went up to the drawing room with Lady Churchill while Sir Winston stayed behind to have a word with Shaw, giving a little wave as he passed to Mrs. Shaw, who had the job of collecting up the reels.

Sometimes when he and I were alone in the cinema watching a film he would turn to me when it ended and say: "Well, what did you think of that?" I usually made a tactful reply, leaving him to give the verdict. If he did not like what he had seen he would grunt one word: "Bloody." If he liked it he used to say, "Remarkable." Nothing else.

One of the films he had shown time and again in the basement cinema was "Lady Hamilton" in which Sir Laurence Olivier played Lord Nelson and Vivien Leigh took the title role. He saw all of Olivier's films, particularly enjoying "Wuthering Heights," "Richard III," and "Hamlet." During the last years of his life, however, it seemed as if he had a special preference for technicolor and on the whole the secretaries were usually on safe ground if they selected colorful adventure films.

An important film that he did *not* see was "Lawrence of Arabia," with Peter O'Toole and a host of other fine actors. There was some technical difficulty over showing this picture because the basement cinema was not geared for such a wide-screen epic. It was a pity. Sir Winston once wrote of Lawrence: "I deem him one of the greatest beings alive in our time. I do not see his like elsewhere. I fear whatever our need we shall never see his like again."

He would have enjoyed seeing the film, having seen Alec Guinness as Lawrence in Terence Rattigan's play, *Ross,* and it would have been interesting to know how he felt about O'Toole's performance. Sir Winston, of course, knew Lawrence well, regarding his death in a motorcycle accident in 1935 as a tremendous blow to the nation.

The films at Chartwell were eagerly looked forward to not only by the great man but also by the staff. There was no social life for us, buried in the Kent countryside, and they helped break up the time we spent there.

The only time films were shown at Sir Winston's London

home was when he was recovering from his broken leg; otherwise they were confined to Chartwell.

He recovered from his back injury amazingly quickly and confounded all the experts because in theory he should have been in a plaster cast. Instead, his will power seemed to drive him to get well again. His recovery was not really the result of any special medical care or treatment; it was sheer determination on his part to be out and about as soon as possible.

His real convalescence took place during the Christmas he spent with his family at Chartwell, and by mid-January 1961 he was able to return to the House of Commons. He loved every minute spent there and was considerably saddened when he had to give up his seat at the 1964 General Election. I don't think he *really* wanted to resign.

The first intimation that he intended going to the House would come after breakfast when he would say: "I think I'll go to the House today." His secretary usually replied, "The doctors advise against it, Sir Winston." We would see his bottom lip jut out and he would reply, "I don't give a damn." He would then consider the matter closed and expect everything to be ready for him to leave for the Commons at 2:30 P.M.

He would set off sitting in the back of his Humber Pullman, his knees wrapped round with a rug. His detective, Murray, sat at the front with the driver. His flag of Lord Warden of the Cinque Ports always flew from the car hood.

The main thing his doctors had against his going to the House was the fact that nonmembers were not allowed in the Chamber. This meant that the detective could not steer Sir Winston to his seat below the gangway, and two members had to be organized to walk with him. He never liked to be seen leaning on their arms, and despite the fact that he had his stick, there was always the fear that he might stumble and fall.

Lady Churchill sided with the doctors, but had to give way when she saw he was set on attending. Everyone agreed that it was the best tonic in the world for Sir Winston to keep going to the Commons because it meant he felt he was still an active parliamentarian.

There was always a crowd at the front of his London home whenever word got round that he might be going out, and tourists would then wait here for hours in the hope of catching a glimpse of him. He was always genuinely pleased to see the crowd waiting for him in the street and, up to the very end, used to give his well-known V-for-Victory sign as he walked the few steps to the car. Once Sir Winston reached the House, he knew that he alone would decide when he left. No one could get at him once he was in the Chamber, and I felt he rather enjoyed this.

When in January 1961 Sir Winston returned to London from Chartwell, he drove to the House of Commons the following day to be welcomed by a wave of cheers. It was the first time he had been in the House since his fall in November, and he was all smiles as he walked, with the aid of a stick, into the Chamber after lunch. His face was flushed with pleasure and his eyes twinkled at the reception. He settled down happily with an Order Paper to hear questions and exchanges about the next week's business. Lord Moran was sitting in the Peers' Gallery keeping an eye on his patient, but he had no need to worry. Sir Winston was fit and well again after an accident that would have put some people out of action for months.

Mr. Hugh Gaitskell, the Opposition leader at that time, was quizzing the Prime Minister, Mr. Harold Macmillan, over some question of UNO, and Mr. Gaitskell was in fact on his feet in the middle of Question Hour when Sir Winston stepped over the line that marks the Bar of the House.

People in the public galleries craned forward to catch a glimpse of the great man and the afternoon's proceedings were momentarily disturbed as Sir Winston took his seat, plugged in his hearing aid, and checked with his neighbor to ask which question had been reached.

After about half an hour the heavy legal business was reached, and he pushed along the front of the Government's Front Bench, shaking hands with Mr. R. A. Butler and nodding to other ministers. After chatting to old friends for a few minutes, he drove back to his London home, happy, no doubt, to be once more in harness.

A few days later Sir Winston went to the Savoy Hotel for a very special occasion: he had Onassis as his guest at the Other Club. Sir Winston founded the club in 1911 with F. E. Smith, later Lord Birkenhead, and the membership list of seventy contains the names of members of Parliament, the House of Lords, the top brass in the Services, and the press barons. The origins of the club are obscure, but one story has it that the club was founded as a place to meet outside the "real club"—the House of Commons. Another insists that the name of the club has no special significance at all.

The club has only three rules: to dine well; not to allow party politics to interfere in any way; and to keep the names of the executive committee members wrapped in impenetrable mystery. The second rule is carried out to the letter. In fact, on one occasion, Sir Winston met and spoke to a member of the Other Club when they were not on speaking terms anywhere else.

As a rule there are no speeches when the club meets in the Pinafore Room, which overlooks the river Thames. But some strange customs and traditions are observed, and one of these concerns a black cat named Kaspar. He is made of wood and is part of the original decor of the room. He was carved from a single piece of plane tree in 1926 and always stands high on a shelf against a carved wall mirror.

He is removed from the shelf only if the club has thirteen sitting down to their meal, being placed on a special chair and treated as a bona fide guest. The place settings are changed before him with each course.

As Sir Winston and Onassis arrived at the Savoy to attend the dinner that night, there was a slight hitch. The manager met them at the Savoy Hill side entrance looking very embarrassed because the passenger elevator was out of service. It did not worry Sir Winston in the slightest. "Come on," he grunted to Onassis and, leaning on his stick, led the way to the service elevator, which took them up to the Pinafore Room.

The menu that night was roast piglet, and there is even a story behind that. The piglet was from the litter of a sow once owned by Sir Winston. The sow was bought by the Mayor of Medicine Hat in Alberta, Canada, at the dispersal sale of Sir Winston's Kent farm. The mayor decided that he would present the great man with one of the sow's piglets and cabled that he was sending one over. The frozen piglet was flown by three planes to London airport and then taken by truck to the Savoy. It was roasted by the chef, Auguste Laplanche, and served with an apple in its mouth. The apple had also been flown over!

Sir Winston always looked forward to attending the dinners, where he met many of his wartime cabinet. He would arrive at the hotel at about 8 P.M., slipping in through the side entrance with a minimum of fuss. And he was invariably the last to leave, shortly before midnight, thoroughly enjoying lingering on over his brandy, coffee and cigar, reminiscing with his old friends.

Sir Winston at this time was still pretty active. He attended the 1961 annual dinner of the Royal Academy, the yearly overture to the Academy's summer exhibition. He went to the Pembroke Theatre, Croydon, to see his daughter Sarah as Rosalind in *As You Like It*. And he was able to get out to fairly frequent dinners in the West End. He seemed to shrug off his eighty-six years, and indeed was able to joke about his age when visitors called to see him. On one occasion when Mr. David Ben-Gurion called at his London home, Sir Winston mentioned that he was "getting on." He beamed when Ben-Gurion replied, "You're not old. Moses lived until he was one hundred and twenty."

Ben-Gurion, with his shock of white hair, was an impressive figure. He radiated personality, so much so that even the slightest contact with him left one in no doubt as to his greatness.

Some people however did not feel kindly about Sir Winston. I remember the shock that spring when we read Malcolm Muggeridge's article about him. It was published in the American magazine *Esquire,* and implied that Sir Winston had been turned into a national monument, which was, Muggeridge wrote, "a sad end to a splendid career." This completely unwarranted attack was duly treated by the Churchills with the contempt it deserved. I do not believe they were really upset by the article; they just chose to ignore it.

Among the many visitors to his Hyde Park Gate home that summer was Lord Avon, one of Sir Winston and Lady Churchill's greatest friends. Lord Avon told them about his decision to accept an earldom. After they left, Sir Winston turned to me and said, "Did you know who that gentleman was?"

He often made this kind of remark after a distinguished guest had departed. I never quite understood why. But then Sir Winston had a lot of curious habits. Another of these was his way of describing the chauffeur. He always called him "The Coachman." It really seems unbelievable now, but that was the name he used. Once I remember

Sir Winston, about to leave his country home for London, asking me, "Is the Coachman on his box?" He was not trying to be funny, nor was he wandering. It may have been the atmosphere down at Chartwell. We had a power cut and candles were being used throughout the house. Maybe the flickering candlelight took him back over the years to the time when he was young.

This nostalgia for the past showed in his love of anything "period." He obviously felt that elegance was missing in his surroundings, despite his love of such modern things as fast travel.

One of the dinners he attended that summer revived many memories. It was of his old regiment, later known as the Queen's Royal Irish Hussars. It took him back more than sixty years to the day in 1895 when, as Lieutenant Churchill, aged twenty, he joined the 4th Hussars from Sandhurst. This sort of occasion really brought home the fantastic life span of the man. The regimental dinner was at Quaglino's, where the ballroom is below street level. To save Sir Winston walking the thirty steps down to the dinner, the Hussars had an industrious upholsterer convert an ordinary service elevator to an elegant one with brown felt on its walls, red carpet on the floor, and two brass pedestal ashtrays in the corners.

Sir Winston walked into the ballroom to meet members of his old regiment, leaning on his walking stick, a present from the deputy Prime Minister of Australia. He was always intensely annoyed at the thought of not being able to get round unaided. But his legs often let him down and there was little he could do about it. It was an object lesson to everyone to see the supreme effort he used to make to lift himself out of deep armchairs and walk unaided from room to room.

Whenever he did this, however, he was taking a chance.

73

He could have stumbled and fallen flat on his face. Out of doors Sir Winston allowed himself to be discreetly guided, especially when we were at airports boarding or leaving planes. Once, when we were at Nice airport returning home to London, he stumbled on the first step of the gangway up to the plane. This was the kind of thing one had to watch for. I remember catching him under both arms as he was falling and lifting him bodily onto the second step. There was a ring of press cameramen standing around us at the time but none of them was fast enough to get a picture, although the fact that he had stumbled was widely reported. At that time he weighed about two hundred and ten pounds. It was a lucky escape.

VII

The Karsh Look

ONE thing I am sure many people did not know
about Sir Winston was that he sang. It was always in a soft,
light voice and not at all like the deep-chested delivery he
had for his famous speeches. He had a large repertoire of
old army barrack-room songs, some of which were slightly
risqué, and these he would often sing when out in the
gardens at Chartwell. The public used to see pictures of
him sitting in contemplative mood overlooking the fishponds and the lake. They probably did not realize that
frequently when he was sitting slumped in his basket chair
like this on the lawns he was singing softly to himself.

He would run the songs together, sometimes mixing
army ballads with a selection from Gilbert and Sullivan,
taking great delight in clearly enunciating the patter songs
from *The Mikado, Pirates of Penzance,* and *HMS Pinafore.* I have heard Sir Winston sing "Burlington Bertie"
and other music-hall songs of the Victorian era. He often
used to make the staff chuckle at the way he reeled off
these songs, but he always had a twinkle in his eye when
he sang them and was fully aware of the fact that he had
an appreciative audience.

Sometimes he would sing snatches of songs to Lady Churchill as they were sitting by the fire after dinner. Other times he recited bits of poetry remembered from his soldiering days. Usually it was Kipling.

Sir Winston was generally expected to lay the foundation stone of Churchill College during the autumn of 1961. When the great day came, however, he was unable to travel to Cambridge. He was quite well, but the journey was considered to be too much for him to undertake and the ceremony, after all, was rather lengthy. That autumn he missed another engagement he badly wanted to keep, but this time it was postponed and he went later in the year. It was "Songs," the annual sing-song at Harrow School. Sir Winston, an old Harrovian, was running a temperature and Lord Moran advised against his going out of doors for a day or two. I know Sir Winston was bitterly disappointed that he could not attend. He was very pleased when he found the whole evening had been postponed until he was better.

That November he was eighty-seven, and most people assumed that he was the oldest member of the House of Commons. This was not the case, however. A veteran Labor M.P., Mr. David Logan, was almost three years older. Yet despite his age, Sir Winston was not nearly as infirm as many people believed. On November 1st, heavily muffled against the cold, he arrived at Quaglino's Restaurant for the coming-out dance of his granddaughter Celia Sandys, then seventeen. The restaurant staff had been told he would only be staying half an hour, but he had such a good time that he did not leave until after midnight.

The occasion was marked by the attendance of practically every member of the Churchill family. Sir Winston, who has seen many a dance step come and go, lightly tapped his foot in time with the music, the Twist. It was the first time it had been played at a débutante dance in

London, and of course during the next year it was to sweep the whole country.

Lady Churchill danced during the evening while Sir Winston talked with his son Randolph, and Miss Sandys' parents, Mr. Duncan Sandys, then Secretary of State for Commonwealth Relations, and Mrs. Diana Sandys, his former wife. Their marriage had been dissolved in 1960.

Sir Winston did not get to bed until 2 A.M., but that morning he was up early and after lunch drove to the House of Commons. In the evening, as if to prove that his batteries were fully recharged after his illness, he went to the Savoy for a dinner of the Other Club. It seems very strange now to recall that in that chair that night was a man who was to be at the center of the biggest scandal of the century: Mr. John Profumo.

I doubt if many men of eighty-seven could have undertaken such a program as Churchill did in three days of that week: Tuesday, State Opening of Parliament; Wednesday, Celia Sandys' coming-out party; Thursday, visit to the Commons and dinner at the Savoy.

His eighty-seventh birthday that year was celebrated quietly at his London home with his son and three daughters attending the dinner party. There was the usual flood of telegrams, parcels, and messages from all over the world.

A few days afterward something happened that passed practically unnoticed. There was a funeral in the West Country that only rated a few lines in the newspapers. Lieutenant Colonel Sir Hugh Bateman Protheroe-Smith died, aged eighty-nine. He and Sir Winston had been officers together in the famous charge of the 21st Lancers against the Dervishes at Omdurman in 1893. His death meant that Sir Winston was the sole surviving officer of the charge.

Little things like this made a deep impression on me, and as I watched Sir Winston busying himself with dinners and other social engagements, I could only marvel at his apparently unlimited energy. At the time the nation was more conscious than ever of the greatness of Sir Winston because the BBC began to rerun "The Valiant Years," while the first run was still unwinding on Saturday nights. It was being repeated in response to the demands of over ten million viewers, many of whom complained that they had missed some of the earlier episodes. The series was one of the most successful ever put on television. I believe it was sold to fourteen countries, including the ex-enemy Japan and, despite what some thought to be a rather brash commentary, Sir Winston seemed to enjoy every minute of it.

There will always be people, I suppose, who imagine that Sir Winston in the last years of his life was completely senile. This was just not true. At eighty-seven he was still attending the House of Commons, often trudging through the division lobby as many as four times in an afternoon in support of the Government.

He was, of course, quite frequently preoccupied with thoughts of the past. After such a life as his, this was no small wonder. And sometimes he would forget a face if he had not seen the person for a long time. But he was very much more "with it" than a lot of people realized.

As I have said, his legs let him down, and at the end he had great difficulty in walking far. The public only saw photographs of him arriving or leaving a place and usually the photographs showed him being assisted. This gave people the idea that he was far more helpless than he actually was.

The old Churchillian spirit was there to the last gasp of his breath. Everyone around him knew he could be as determined as ever when he wished. On the days we saw the "Karsh look," we knew we were in for trouble. The "Karsh look" was the expression we used whenever

Churchill's bottom lip jutted out in dogged determination; when he looked as he did in the famous wartime photograph taken by the Canadian photographer. Karsh got his world-famous picture by one simple move: he pulled his sitter's cigar from his mouth just before taking the picture. Sir Winston glowered, the camera clicked, and the greatest portrait of the man was recorded.

Whenever Sir Winston had this look on his face, it was best to let him do exactly what he wanted. I never fancied tangling with him once I saw that bottom lip forcefully protruded. I remember seeing the expression on one occasion when Lady Churchill told him to stop poking the fire with his walking stick, something he was always doing.

We saw the "Karsh look" turned on as he continued to stir the embers. He took no notice of his wife. This was unusual because, on the whole, Lady Churchill was the one person who could tell her husband what he should do and get results. Many times, when he was late for meals and the guests were arriving at the front door, an appeal had to be made to Lady Churchill to tell her husband to bestir himself.

Sir Winston in a temper was something I shall not easily forget. It seemed as if he could cope with the big things in life while little ones drove him frantic. I saw the "Karsh look" very early during a visit to the Riviera. Sir Winston was irritated at my not moving fast enough to get something for him in his bedroom and threw a pair of hairbrushes at me shouting, "Move, Howes! Goddammit, move!" The brushes whistled past my head and hit the bedroom door.

On the other hand, he never let the sun go down on his wrath and at times showed flashes of generosity. When his horse won a big race, he gave me a check for fifty pounds. I was very moved. Another time he paid for the wife of a recently married member of the staff to fly out to the south of France to join her husband for a holiday. Then there were the times when he would shyly hold out a couple of books and mumble, "I'd like you to have these." They would be autographed copies of his wartime speeches or memoirs. He never gave books as presents out of condescension. He genuinely thought they would make a nice present for someone who had given special service.

The months flew by quickly when one was with him. When he was in London he spent most of his time at Hyde Park Gate, content to receive a steady flow of visitors, entertaining them at lunch or dinner. But occasionally he made forays into the West End to attend special functions, and one of the most memorable of these was the dinner party given by Lord Rothermere on May 25, 1962, to celebrate the eighty-third birthday of Lord Beaverbrook.

All the leading newspaper proprietors were at Warwick House that evening as Lord Rothermere, chairman of Associated Newspapers, received his guests. Sir Winston and Mr. Harold Macmillan attended as lifelong friends and wartime colleagues of Lord Beaverbrook, who had been Minister of Aircraft Production during the war. Mr. Macmillan had been Beaverbrook's Parliamentary Secretary at the Ministry of Supply.

The great crystal chandelier in the superb first-floor Grinling Gibbons drawing room of Lord Rothermere's home shone down as he received his guests, and a special place was found for Sir Winston as soon as he arrived. Photographers took a group picture of the company before they sat down to dinner, and Lord Rothermere had his guests group themselves round the settee on which sat Lord Beaverbrook, flanked by Sir Winston and Mr. Macmillan.

The highlight of the party was the presentation to Lord Beaverbrook of a two-foot-wide solid silver gallery tea tray, engraved with the signature of every guest. It was a night to remember, certainly one that Sir Winston thoroughly enjoyed. When the company sat down to dinner at the long inlaid mahogany table, he sat on Beaverbrook's right, turning up the volume of his hearing aid to make sure that he did not miss one word of the conversation. He was very thrilled to be at the party in honor of the man he knew simply as "Max." Theirs was a lasting friendship, and the two men were never closer than they were on that memorable occasion.

VIII

"Toby, come down here—at once!"

Sɪʀ Wɪɴsᴛᴏɴ loved animals. He was extremely gentle with them, talking to them as he stroked them. There were his poodles, Rufus One and Rufus Two, and a marmalade cat named Ginger, all buried at Chartwell. And toward the end of his life he had a kitten called Jock. But of all the pets Sir Winston ever had, none was more loved than Toby.

Toby was a green parakeet, given to Sir Winston as a present. He was very tame and would fly round the room when let out of his cage. He slept in Sir Winston's bedroom in the cage, which stood near the window on a stand. Whenever Sir Winston was in bed and awake, the cage was taken off the stand and put on the bed at his side.

When the breakfast tray was brought in, Toby would sit on its edge and peck at Sir Winston's grapefruit. Then Toby would move on to the main course, usually steak or bacon and eggs, leaving Sir Winston to eat round him. It was something quite fascinating to watch! Here was this great man sitting up in bed eating his breakfast with a parakeet pecking away all over his tray. Whenever Sir Winston had grapefruit or tinned pineapple (which he preferred), he left a little for Toby to finish off. Toby, of course, had been eating steadily through the meal anyway and by this time had usually moved on to stage two, spreading the toothpicks. These were in a narrow glass on the tray, and Toby used to pick them out one by one, carry them to the side of the tray, and drop them onto the counterpane. After this he usually hopped onto his master's saucer and tipped his coffee spoon off the tray.

Once breakfast was over, Toby used to fly to the bedside table and quite deliberately keep tapping the various articles on it until they were edged off and fell on the floor. Invariably the matches spilled, and when the time came to clear up there was a considerable amount of debris scattered around the bed: cigar-piercer, paper-knife, matches, knick-knacks, quite a collection. All the time this was going on, Sir Winston would be reading the morning newspapers. Occasionally Toby rounded off his morning show by fluttering his wings in an overflowing ashtray, showering everyone, and everything, with ash.

If anyone came into the room, Toby would fly over and perch on his head. Members of the staff often had to carry on with their duties around Sir Winston with Toby on top. It was impossible to shoo the bird away for fear of offending him, and there were times when a secretary would be taking dictation with Toby busy biting at her ear. Letters, when they were about to be signed, were often found to have a ragged edge at the top of the page: Toby's work. If the letter was an important one, it was retyped; if it was to a member of the family or close friend, it was sent off as it was.

Both Sir Winston and Lady Churchill belonged to the local public library, and there was always a small pile of library books at his bedside. Toby even pecked at the pages of the library books. There must have been a lot of people in the borough of Kensington and at Westerham who were puzzled by the ragged pages of the books they took out from the library.

Toby had his cage cleaned out every day and was bathed twice a week. He traveled all over the world with Sir Winston, and ordering his supply of seed, sandpaper, parakeet grit, spray, cuttlefish, tonic seed, and bill of health from the vet every time we went abroad, was almost as important as ordering the cigars.

At lunchtime Toby was taken down to the dining room and allowed to fly about during the midday meal. Usually he was allowed out only during the coffee, but if Sir Winston and Lady Churchill had no guests, Toby flew around during the whole meal. He usually caused quite a stir, fluttering about the table, knocking over glasses and salt cellars.

Parakeets always seem to go the same way in the end: out of the window. And that is what occurred in Toby's case. It happened when we were in the south of France staying at the Hotel de Paris in Monte Carlo. Sir Winston was in bed one morning when the secretary came in. Toby as usual was sitting on the bed table. But after walking in from the lounge the secretary left the salon door open.

Toby had never flown through the salon door before, always confining his flying to one room, even though the door might be open. But for some reason that day he decided to fly straight through the open salon door and out of the French windows. We were on the eighth floor and a strong cross wind blew him straight into the park below the hotel. We all gave chase and eventually found him perched on the branch of a tree eight feet from the ground.

Mr. Montague Brown, Sir Winston's secretary, stood under the tree with the cage and in stern tones warned the erring bird, "Toby, come down here—*at once!*" Toby took no notice, but a lot of the French people standing around did. It all smacked of "Mad dogs and Englishmen," and I felt that behind my back the French and Monagasques were thinking that here was an example of typically English behavior.

One of the commissionaires came running from the hotel with a ladder, which he propped against the tree. This immediately disturbed Toby, who flew away down a small side street into the main park outside Monte Carlo's Casino. Again we all chased after him but it was no use. The park was full of starlings and Toby had vanished among them.

We left the cage at the foot of the trees in the park for days. But Toby never returned. Sir Winston was heartbroken. Offers of parakeets poured in from all over the world when the story got out that he had been lost. Toby was never replaced.

Sir Winston tried to console himself with Onassis' parakeet, but it was a much smaller bird with less character. Onassis presented it in the hope that it would cheer up Sir Winston on his return to England.

The bird's name was Byron. He was a vicious little thing that would bite and draw blood. Sir Winston tried hard to accept Byron, but it really had little appeal after his beloved Toby. Asked what he thought of Byron, Sir Winston said, "He's all right, but it's not Toby." Lord Montgomery attempted to reform Byron and took him away for a special course. It did not seem to work because we never saw the bird again.

Rufus One and Rufus Two, the poodles, were great favorites of Sir Winston, as was the marmalade cat kept permanently at Chartwell. The runner-up to Toby in Sir Winston's eyes was undoubtedly a ginger kitten presented to him in February 1964 by Mr. Jock Colville, his private secretary during the war.

Mr. Colville came to dinner one evening and over the

soup course mentioned that Sir Winston was without a pet. "Why don't you get another?" he asked. "You should have another animal. If I gave you a kitten would you accept it?" Sir Winston beamed and said, "Indeed I would."

A few days later Mr. Colville arrived at the house in London carrying a small cardboard box. He took it straight into the drawing room, put it down on a table, and told Sir Winston, "I've brought you this kitten." Churchill named the kitten Jock on the spot. It was from an R.S.P.C.A. clinic and had no pedigree. Mr. Colville had rescued it from being destroyed.

In no time at all the kitten had left great scratches on Sir Winston's hands and arms. He did not seem to mind the pain, and in all fairness one could not really blame the kitten, which was being hugged rather roughly. The kitten was often completely lost in a cloud of cigar smoke and must have wondered what kind of home he had come to.

Sir Winston used to say, "Oh you *are* a beautiful pussy-cat. You really are." If the kitten struggled he would grasp it even more tightly and say gruffly, "Oh, don't go now."

He did the same thing with Ginger at Chartwell, but, being bigger, Ginger usually managed to free himself, angrily shake his fur, and stalk haughtily out of the room.

Jock, on the other hand, never managed to escape the great man's clutches. He was extremely popular with his master and always traveled with him whenever he went to Chartwell. It was there that he was knocked down by a car in the road outside the house.

Fortunately he was found by a young boy who was passing on a bicycle and taken to the gardener's cottage. When we saw him we thought he was going to die, and, in all probability, had he been an *ordinary* cat he would have been put to sleep. Sir Winston was naturally very upset and the vet was called in immediately. He took Jock away to his office, escorted by one of Sir Winston's staff, and wired up the kitten's smashed jaw.

The kitten caught pneumonia, and for a while it was uncertain whether it would live. But with careful attention he pulled round, growing from a tiny ginger kitten into a very large cat. He was with Sir Winston to the end and gave him a great deal of pleasure. Sir Winston was so fond of Jock that he went to great lengths to save the kitten's life on another occasion when he had a stomach upset and developed canker of the ear. The veterinary surgeon's bill on that occasion came to over thirty pounds. The death of a pet, as someone once said, adds a pang to life. And I know that Sir Winston was terribly upset whenever he lost one.

The two poodles always ran loose both at Chartwell and Hyde Park Gate, never being confined to any one room. In the latter years, when Sir Winston was traveling abroad a lot, Rufus Two (who replaced Rufus One) was always left at home, spending most of his time in the care of Miss Grace Hamblin, Lady Churchill's private secretary.

Once, at Chartwell, when the dog came into the drawing room, Sir Winston bent down to stroke it. Rufus Two suddenly shot away when he saw Miss Hamblin passing the door. Sir Winston shook his head and said sadly, "He doesn't love me any more." Thereafter he paid little attention to Rufus; with Sir Winston it was a case of all or nothing.

Before he alienated Rufus Two's attention by spending long spells abroad, the poodle either slept at the bottom of his bed, or in the next room on an armchair. He was the poodle that trotted into the bedroom every morning and woke Sir Winston by licking his face. Whenever Sir Winston slept late, the staff had to make sure Rufus was taken out for his morning run. The pets all had special collars and identification discs that read, "Churchill, Hyde Park Gate."

A Siamese cat was one of the many house cats at Chartwell, and on one occasion was imprudent enough to give his master a deep scratch on the hand. Sir Winston did the only thing: he threw the cat out the front door to teach it a lesson. It completely disappeared, and Sir Winston was very upset. Filled with remorse, he wanted to put an advertisement in the "Lost and Found" columns of the Westerham local newspaper. But before he could do this, the cat turned up on the front doorstep after being away four days.

Sir Winston, greatly relieved, was a different man. He made great play of fetching the Siamese a saucer of milk, although the cat was not really starving. Wherever it had been it had obviously eaten well. Sir Winston was the kind of man who would never say he was sorry for something he had done, preferring instead to try and make up for any bad feeling by deed rather than word. This applied to humans as well as animals.

Another pet at his country home was Ginger, the marmalade cat. He was very popular but unfortunately tended to molt rather a lot. This would not have mattered had Sir Winston not been fond of picking him up and playing with him. He occasionally did this before dinner and Ginger would cover him with hairs. I always had to be hovering with a clothes brush whenever this happened, making sure that Sir Winston did not walk into the dining room to meet his guests with cat's hairs all over his dinner jacket. It would not have worried him in the least had he done this; he always regarded my attempts to keep him tidy as rather unnecessary. "Oh leave it!" he would say. "I'm all right as I am, stop brushing me down."

Ginger always seemed to enjoy the comfort of the armchairs in the basement cinema and was constantly being moved out by the staff. Important guests would later be seen with their trousers covered with his hairs, after they had inadvertently sat in the chair he had been sleeping on.

A badger, knocked down outside the gates of Chartwell by Sir Winston's car, caused him great distress. Badgers apparently cry when on the point of death, and this particular one made a considerable noise. It cried real tears as it died. It was later sent to a taxidermist to be skinned. The skin was then mounted on a square of red velvet and hung in Sir Winston's bedroom on the door of his built-in sliding wardrobe.

One night when Sir Winston was about to climb into bed he paused, looked across at the badger's skin and said, "I knocked him down, you know. And he cried. He really did."

Another time, when Sir Winston was passing the mounted head of a fox, presented by a local hunt, he patted it and commented, "Poor fox." Little things like that were typical of him. He even had strong feelings about bees, wasps, or moths that flew into the bedroom, never allowing anyone to kill them while he was there. "Make sure you put him out of the window," he would say.

IX

"You monsters, leave me alone!"

Oɴᴇ mishap that gained worldwide publicity was the occasion when Sir Winston broke a leg in the summer of 1962. There were many different reports and most of them were wrong. I know exactly what happened because I was on the spot, and it may be worthwhile recounting the affair in some detail.

He had been on the Riviera only two days when he fell, fracturing his left leg, in his eighth-floor suite at the Hotel de Paris, Monte Carlo. It happened just before breakfast. A New Zealand nurse, Miss Robin Powell, was on duty and was sitting outside Sir Winston's room reading a book when she heard a crash and a thud in the bedroom.

She ran in and found Sir Winston lying on the floor alongside his enormous double bed. An hour before she had looked in and seen him asleep and, having no reason to suspect anything, she had returned to her book. At that time he used to call out if he wanted assistance. He had an electric bell with a buzzer that rang outside, but although this push-button warning system was always pinned to his sheets to stop it falling off his bed, he never bothered to use it.

On this occasion he decided to get out of bed by himself to make his way to the bathroom. He evidently could see the light shining under the door to the anteroom where Nurse Powell was sitting and, mistaking this for the bathroom, slowly walked toward it in the dark.

When he reached it he realized that it was the wrong door and, turning sharply, collided with the bedside table. While he was walking toward the light shining under the door, the furniture was in silhouette. Turning to retrace his footsteps meant that he was walking into complete darkness as there was no light from the windows, sealed on the outside by heavy steel shutters after the fashion of a venetian blind.

The crash Nurse Powell heard was the noise of the angle-poised lamp being knocked off the glass-topped side table. The thud was Sir Winston hitting the floor. A heavy carpet was fitted in the bedroom and Nurse Powell could obviously not have heard Sir Winston moving about. Nor was there any question of her proper place being in the room with him. He insisted on sleeping in complete darkness and it would have been asking a lot of a nurse to sit in the darkened bedroom all night without falling asleep.

The first thing Nurse Powell did was ring for me. I was asleep on the third floor. I told her to telephone Sir Winston's secretary and Dr. Roberts, who lived at Cap d'Ail, two miles away. Hurriedly dressing, I ran upstairs to Sir Winston's suite. I found him lying on the floor in his bedroom, covered by a blanket and with his head propped up by a mound of pillows. He seemed reasonably calm and, smiling benignly, said, "I think I've hurt my leg." When it came to suffering pain, I knew he was remarkably strong. If anything, his weakness was anticipating pain.

A great wave of depression swept over me as I realized the possible repercussions of the accident. Sir Winston, despite all the constant care and attention to see that he came to no harm, had fallen and broken his left leg. I knew what this could lead to, further complications that did not bear thinking about.

I looked at him lying propped up on the bedroom floor and thought how relaxed he looked. His face was not lined with pain as one might have expected. I remembered that he had once said, "All babies look like me," and, as he lay there on the carpet, I realized it was quite true. His face had no really prominent features; it was exactly as he described it.

Naturally the news of his fall spread rapidly. It was not exactly something that could be kept quiet, especially in a French hotel. Unknown to me, a local news agency put out a report that I had been with Sir Winston when he fell and as a result the world's newspapers gave the impression that I was to blame! When I discovered this I felt even more depressed; it seemed just about the most disastrous thing that could happen to me. Fortunately, those around Sir Winston knew the true position and realized that no one could have averted the accident.

Dr. Roberts arrived at the hotel, and after a brief examination telephoned the Princess Grace Clinic just outside the town and asked them to rush over a portable X-ray unit. It was set up in the bedroom half an hour later, and Dr. André Fissore, who headed the unit, took a series of X-rays. The plates confirmed that the fracture was in the upper third of the femur.

Sir Winston, still lying on the floor, was made as comfortable as possible. Dr. Roberts put his leg in a splint, and by the time the ambulancemen got up to the eighth floor, the whole of the hotel knew about the accident. The speed with which the news traveled amazed me. All the doors to the suite were locked and Murray, the detective, was stationed outside in the corridor.

As Sir Winston was wheeled to the hotel elevator, dozens

of maids and hotel staff gathered in the corridors. The elevator was too small to take the stretcher, so Sir Winston had to be carried down to the ground floor. He was quite a weight, and the stretcher-bearers and I had to take rests on the stairs. We carried him out of the rear door of the hotel, and I remember him smiling and waving to a small crowd as he went. Two French newspapermen saw him put in the ambulance, but the photographers were nowhere to be seen.

I understood why ten minutes later, after a hectic drive to the clinic. An army of pressmen were waiting outside the main doors of the hospital, which stands on a hill overlooking the town.

The clinic, opened three years earlier by Prince Rainier and Princess Grace, had its operating room on the fourth floor. Everything had been prepared as soon as the hospital got the news of the fall.

Sir Winston was whisked up in the elevator, put on a trolley, and wheeled into a private side room. An hour later he was taken to the operating room and given an injection. At that time Lady Churchill was in England, and after an urgent telephone call to her, the doctors announced that Lord Moran had said the operation should be carried out in London where he would be in attendance.

It was agreed that a temporary hip-to-heel immobilizing plaster should be put on the leg to prevent movement and any complications of the fracture. Working under Professor Charles Chatelin, the surgeons very slowly set the leg and put on plaster. After about an hour Sir Winston was wheeled back to his room.

I was at his bedside when he came round from the anesthetic. It took him a minute or two to focus on the doctors' faces leaning over him. Then, trying to lift himself up in bed, he roared in typical Churchillian fashion,

"You monsters! You monsters! Leave me alone. Get out of here—all of you!"

He was furious when he discovered that he was in plaster, and soon made it clear that he strongly resented the fact. It was obvious that he had declared open war on the doctors. Everything they decided, he opposed. Everything the nurses brought to his bedside, he waved away. The hospital corridors echoed with Churchillian epithets as he bellowed at everyone who came near him. The French doctors and nurses must have been slightly taken aback at the fireworks, but the English team around him were used to it.

At seven o'clock that evening he had a light meal and the inevitable brandy and cigar. The French doctors advised against the brandy and cigar, but there was little they could do to stop Sir Winston having them.

Before leaving the hotel bedroom I had hastily stuffed a small suitcase with the essentials: a bottle of brandy, a bottle of whisky, soda water, a box of mixed cigars, his special Canadian matches, and, as an afterthought, a bottle of sleeping tablets, which were never used. It seems ridiculous now, but, at the time, all these things except the tablets were essential to his recovery.

The British nursing team completely took over from the French hospital staff in looking after his immediate needs. Few of the French nurses spoke English, and it was considered better to keep the familiar team with Sir Winston rather than surround him with people he was not used to. He did not like new faces. Indeed every time I left him to go off duty he would ask, "Why?" One can appreciate the effect this kind of remark had on a new nurse about to take over. He strongly resented the nursing team changing round. Among his favorite female nurses was Sister Glenda McAlpin, the pretty redheaded Australian girl, who had been a driver-hostess at the Melbourne Olympics.

94

Sir Winston had an affinity for redheads. After all, he had been one himself.

Sir Winston in bed with a broken leg was bad enough, but things became rather chaotic when we found we were fighting a running battle with the French press photographers. They tried every trick imaginable to get through to Room 102. Some disguised themselves as hospital orderlies, others as doctors, to slip past Murray and his reinforcements, uniformed Monagasque policemen and plain-clothed French detectives.

One of the French photographers even got as far as the stairs. I saw a smartly dressed man wearing an old raincoat and carrying a plumber's bag of tools. He did not quite look the part and I pointed him out. The tool bag was opened and inside we found cameras, film, and long-distance lenses. The photographer had nearly beaten us and was only a few yards from Sir Winston's door.

The photographers next tried climbing a tree outside Sir Winston's balcony, but they were spotted and brought down. They tried every trick in the book. It was like being in a goldfish bowl. Everywhere one looked there were photographers with those long-range cameras that look like submachine guns. They used to sit in the courtyard under his window, and whenever anyone went near the bedroom windows they would all jump to their feet and frantically start taking pictures.

All the time, messages and telegrams were pouring into the hospital from all over the world. The Queen and Prince Philip sent a get-well message and there was a telegram from Prince Rainier and Princess Grace.

Because of the crowds that would be attracted if it were generally known when he was leaving the hospital, the decision on the exact time and day of departure for England was left to the last moment. As a result I had to tear round frantically shoving everything into suitcases only a short while before the plane took off.

The day after the fall, Sir Winston left the hospital on a stretcher, one of his cigars wedged in his mouth. The hospital staff crowded at the windows to watch the departure of their most famous patient, who waved and smiled at them as we put him into the ambulance. He was in fine form and showed no signs of the pain he must have been suffering.

He had a tremendous send-off. Nurses, patients, doctors, domestic staff, men in overalls and boiler suits, people from nearby houses, all turned out to wave goodbye. The crowd clapped when they saw Sir Winston carried out and there were cries of "Bon voyage!" This kind of thing gave him a great lift and helped his subsequent recovery enormously.

Dr. Roberts sat in the back of the small ambulance with his patient, and I sat in front with the driver. As we drove the thirteen miles of twisting Riviera road to Nice airport, a French TV camera team drove in front of us, shooting their film from the top of their truck. We were doing about fifty miles an hour on the winding roads, and the truck was only a car length in front. As if this was not enough, a small Citroen kept buzzing past us, photographers leaning out of the window to take pictures. As it was a closed-in ambulance, they got little for their trouble.

By this time, however, we had all ceased to be surprised at the antics of the French press. If one of their photographers had climbed onto the hood of the ambulance as we sped along, it would not have amazed me. It was quite a motorcade. French police motorcyclists were in front to clear a way, then the TV truck, followed by Sir Winston's ambulance. Behind this was a car full of detectives, another car with secretaries and, bringing up the rear, the rest of Sir Winston's staff.

Mr. Macmillan, then Prime Minister, had personally

arranged for his old friend to fly home in an R.A.F. Comet ambulance. We left Nice airport at 11 A.M. and a special team of R.A.F. nurses looked after Sir Winston during the flight. On the way over the Channel he showed signs of impatience, twice asking the crew, "How much longer are we going to be?" The Comet flew at 10,000 feet lower than usual so that the cabin pressure would be reduced and Sir Winston would have an easier time breathing.

He sipped weak whisky and coffee provided by the steward, who also made tea for the rest of the passengers. We could see that the effects of the accident were beginning to tell, because although Sir Winston had appeared cheerful and confident when he boarded the aircraft at Nice, he was obviously feeling the strain at the end of the flight. Yet he did not complain once; it was if he was determined to show us all once more his remarkable capacity for withstanding pain. He simply was not prepared to give in.

At London Airport Lady Churchill, Randolph, and Lord Moran were waiting to meet the invalid. A fork-lift truck carefully lowered him down to the pavement and he was put straight into an ambulance and taken to the Middlesex Hospital. The journey into London was most touching because every time the ambulance was caught up in a traffic jam, people ran into the road, tapped on the ambulance windows, and shouted out, "Get well soon, Sir Winston!"

By the time we got to the side entrance of the Middlesex, the street was jammed with people and the ambulance had slowly to carve a way through. He received a fantastic reception when he was carried out giving his familiar V-sign. We all felt glad he was home but were rather apprehensive about how the fall would affect his health. Sir Winston, at eighty-seven, had amazed the doctors on the Riviera with the way he had withstood the manipulative operation.

Any other person of his age, having broken his leg, would not have been able to manage the trip, but Sir Winston was in such shape that the doctors operated as soon as he arrived at the Middlesex.

Within thirty-six hours he had two general anesthetics. I should be surprised if a broken limb has ever caused such comings and goings before. It demonstrated the incredible interest the whole world took in the health of a particular man.

X

"I won't take those today, thank you!"

THE Middlesex Hospital, I am sure, did not fully
realize what they were taking on when Sir Winston arrived
in an ambulance, replying to the crowds' cheers with his
wonderfully flamboyant thumbs-up sign. He certainly arrived in plenty of style, and we had to smile when the
hospital announced that he was going to be treated "as
just another patient." It seemed that this important piece
of information never reached him. Just another patient
indeed! How could he be? As usual, he carried on doing
everything he was supposed not to do.

There was no doubt about it, his powers of recovery
were remarkable. Few men of the same age could have
withstood such a battering as he went through. The broken
leg led to bronchitis, which led to pneumonia, which led
to a thrombosis a week later. Then, a week after that he
had jaundice. He surely made medical history.

He simply ploughed on as if all this were normal routine, smoking his usual number of cigars, seven or eight
a day, drinking brandy and whisky exactly as he did at
home. The routine was the same, champagne with his
meals, a brandy afterward, and whiskies in between. But

he never believed in drinking on an empty stomach and perhaps this was his big secret. Eating without drinking champagne was out of the question for him, and right to the end he drank it with every meal.

It gives one some idea of his resilience when one considers that within an hour of his arrival at the Middlesex Hospital he was in the operating room. And this was after a flight from Nice Airport and less than thirty-six hours after his fall in the hotel.

Sir Winston was put in a first-floor room of the special private patients wing in the Woolavington wing. His bed was specially angled so that he could look out onto the peaceful and secluded garden with its goldfish in an ornamental pond. The hospital wing was given by Lord Woolavington, the famous racehorse owner, in memory of his wife.

The Middlesex is proud that Florence Nightingale was once one of its nurses. England's first woman doctor, Elizabeth Barrett Anderson, also studied there eighty years before the hospital agreed to admit women students to its Medical School.

When Sir Winston was wheeled into his hospital room, he found it filled with flowers sent by family friends and admirers. A special show of yellow irises, blue delphiniums, carnations, and stocks stood alongside his bed. People passing the hospital kept dropping in to ask the man at the enquiry desk, "How is he?" There was no mistaking who they were inquiring about.

Lord Moran, Professor Herbert Seddon, and Mr. Philip Newman studied the X-ray plates and then carried out the hour-long operation. The professor was consultant orthopedic surgeon of the Royal National Orthopedic Hospital, and Mr. Newman was senior consultant orthopedic surgeon at the Middlesex. After the operation Lady Churchill was

Sir Winston's first visitor. She found him cheerful but a little drowsy.

The fame of Professor Seddon is international. He holds many honors in orthopedic and nerve surgery and is also an expert on polio. Mr. Newman, a Harley Street consultant, was a hero of Dunkirk. He was on the beaches with the wounded and cheerfully accepted a ballot that meant he was left in charge of the casualties and was not able to be taken off the beach.

As Mr. Newman left the Middlesex immediately after the operation, there was a considerable crowd waiting in the street. He put their minds at rest, telling them: "The old man's quite all right."

Two days after the operation Sir Winston developed bronchitis. The doctors were not unduly worried and no doubt expected as much after the events of the previous few days. But, just as everyone thought it was clearing up, he developed congestion of the lungs. The morning they discovered this, he was propped up in bed smoking one of his giant cigars. When Lord Moran tried to examine him, he found Sir Winston unwilling to part with the cigar, wedged firmly between his teeth. As usual he had a great deal of trouble persuading him to part with it so that he could listen to his chest with his stethoscope.

It was very hard at this time to persuade Sir Winston to take the pills prescribed by his doctors. He just did not like them. Whenever he was handed pills, he would politely hand them back saying, "No, I won't take those today, thank you." It was the same with injections. Sir Winston would say one word, "No." That was that. No injection was given.

The most depressing thing about nursing him was when the doctors would give their instructions and then leave me to it. Lord Moran would say, "Continue the antibiotics, Howells; I shall be in tomorrow." He would then leave and my heart would sink as I looked at the determined expression on my patient's face.

It seems remarkable that Sir Winston was sitting in a chair and in such high spirits two days after the surgeons had pinned the fractured ends of his leg together. He ate well and was very cheerful when Lady Churchill and other visitors called. Among the "visitors" was a full Salvation Army band that marched alongside the hospital one afternoon playing "Onward Christian Soldiers" with great gusto. The band formed up outside the side entrance and continued with a selection of hymns, despite large notices prominently displayed saying, "Hospital, quiet please." Sir Winston thoroughly enjoyed it.

As one might have expected, the letters poured in again and an army of pressmen camped outside the hospital, which is just off Oxford Street. The hospital superintendent set aside the oak-paneled board room for the reporters, even supplying them with tea, coffee, and biscuits. The reporters got together to send Sir Winston a box of his favorite cigars with the message, "Good wishes from the pressmen downstairs to whom news of your progress has been of more than purely professional concern." Sir Winston was an ex-newspaperman after all, and he was very touched. The final complication was a mild phlebitis in his leg, but it did not really hamper his recovery.

Part of the plan to keep him entertained in his small room was to show films, and several were sent round by a film company. We had "Winchester 73," a Western; "Above Us the Waves," a naval drama; "Genevieve," the comedy about a veteran car; "The Vanishing Prairie," a Disney film; "The Wooden Horse," about the P.O.W. camp escape; and "The Battle of the River Plate." These were just the kind of films he liked.

So many gifts arrived at the hospital that his secretarial staff were called in to help deal with them. One of the presents was from the landlady of a nearby public house. She sent a clockwork model of a barman drinking brandy and blowing smoke through his ears. It caused considerable amusement.

Sir Winston remained cheerful as usual, puffing away at his cigars, drinking his brandies, and generally acting as if nothing was wrong with him. When his son, Randolph, called he was sitting up in bed, sipping a stiff brandy and wiggling his toes. Randolph told him that he would be back to visit him, and his indomitable father replied, "I hope that you will see me in the House of Commons."

Two weeks after his operation he was well enough to have several of the stitches removed from his leg. The week after this he began walking. A chair was placed across the room from his bed and gingerly, with a physiotherapist at his side, he walked over to it. The next day he walked thirty yards in the hospital corridor. It was a great credit not only to the doctors and nurses but also to Sir Winston himself. Once more he had overcome a severe disability by his sheer determination.

Each day I reported for duty at 11 P.M. and found my patient sitting up in bed reading. A mound of six pillows supported him. Even in the hospital he still read an enormous amount, refusing to turn out his bedside light before midnight. The conversation between us would be brief but to the point.

"Oh, Howes. There you are at last."

"I hear you were walking today, Sir Winston."

"Uh . . . yes . . . uh . . . I think I did very well."

"Did you find it painful?"

"Uh . . . uh . . . uh . . . no. No, not really."

This was typical. He never complained about the pain he must have been feeling. Nor do I remember him grousing about the boredom of lying in bed all day.

At this stage Sir Winston could have gone home at any time, but the alterations to Hyde Park Gate were taking longer than had been expected. His bedroom was moved to a ground-floor room, which had to be decorated. And a new bathroom had to be put in with special handrails. We knew he would insist on his daily baths.

His appetite was not diminished by the accident. He always enjoyed his meals, and in the hospital he tucked into things like asparagus soup, caviar, fricassee of chicken, omelettes, strawberry ice cream, cheese, and biscuits with great relish. Always there was the small bottle of champagne on his meal tray and the bottle of old brandy at his bedside. If one of the nursing team attempted to pour him a brandy he would say, "No. Leave it. *I* do the pouring." He loved his brandy and never dispensed it lightly.

"Would you like a little of this?" he would ask me.

"I'd love some, Sir Winston. It is most kind of you," I would reply, knowing that I was being highly honored.

Sir Winston invariably said, "This is a very good brandy, you know." It always was, of course. He knew his brandies.

"You must learn to savor it properly," he once told me. "It is something to take one's time over. Water? I never believe in adding water to brandy. That is a great crime. Fine old brandy is something to be treasured. Never forget that."

The hospital made very elaborate arrangements to look after him. Apart from myself and the two female private nurses, the Middlesex had a team of three sisters, three staff nurses, and two other nurses. We all worked well together. Murray used to patrol up and down the corridor keeping a watchful eye on everyone who went into the bedroom. Every time a visitor left, the reporters crowded round the hospital doors to find out the latest news, but both they and the cameramen behaved with much more restraint than those we had encountered at the Princess Grace Clinic.

Sir Winston left the hospital on the morning of August 21st. As he was carried in a chair by four attendants to an L.C.C. ambulance that was waiting at a side entrance, hundreds of people jammed the street to cheer him on his way. The hospital windows and those of nearby offices were crammed and there were even people on the hospital roof.

Completely in his element, he waved to the crowd, held tightly back by policemen standing shoulder to shoulder. Puffing at his cigar and smiling, he kept waving as dozens of onlookers broke through the ranks and ran toward him. They saw the famous V-sign as the attendants lifted him into the ambulance and closed the doors. I sat next to him as we slowly weaved a path through the pressing crowds. It was a very emotional scene. Women were weeping and people were shouting out, "Good old Winnie!" and, "Bless you, sir, get well soon!"

The day before the departure, the family Humber had picked up the apparatus he used to exercise his leg. It was a set of portable parallel bars on a wooden base that gave him support when he practiced walking. Within two days, however, these had been discarded and he was able to walk from his bedroom to the drawing room with the aid of his stick and the special handrail that had been fitted along the corridor wall.

For his return home Sir Winston was immaculately turned out. He wore his gray homburg, initialed W.S.C. on the silk lining, his gold cuff links engraved with the family crest on one side and his monogram on the other, a cream poplin collar-attached shirt, and a medium gray Prince of Wales check suit with knife-edge creases in the trousers. He wore a blue polka-dot tie, and across his six-button waistcoat hung his heavy gold watch-chain. His watch was in the left-hand bottom waistcoat pocket and at the other end of the chain was an interesting little assortment.

They were all very small items, each with its own sentimental value. There was a minute gold snuffbox, a gold penknife, a gold cigar piercer, a ruby set in a gold heart given to him by Lady Churchill on their engagement, and a gold circle enclosing a V-for-Victory sign. All Sir Winston's wartime staff have one of these, treasuring them as personal mementos of Sir Winston.

He had only been home a short while when some sad news was broken to him. Rufus Two, his black poodle, had died at Chartwell while he was in hospital. The news had been kept from him in case it might upset him. They were great friends, and the dog had been with the family fifteen years, replacing Rufus One, who was run over by a bus in Brighton during the 1947 Conservative Conference. He was given as a present by a Canadian magazine publisher, and although Sir Winston was always being presented with a menagerie of pets, Rufus Two was a firm favorite. He was a frequent visitor to Party conferences, and every time he went for a trim he made news.

XI

Back Home

Sɪʀ Wɪɴsᴛᴏɴ was home again. He celebrated his
return by calling all the staff into his bedroom for a glass
of champagne. However, this did not mean that our troubles were over!

His bedroom was now on the ground floor, and it was
decided that rather than have him negotiate the corridor
and winding staircase down to the dining room, he should
take all his meals in a small anteroom off his bedroom.

That was the plan. But, like so many plans made for Sir
Winston, it did not work in practice. He had no idea of
taking things easy after breaking his leg at eighty-seven.
After having two meals in the anteroom, one of them with
Lord Beaverbrook, who dropped in for lunch shortly after
his return, he decided that he did not care for eating there.
Much to everyone's alarm, he insisted on eating in the
dining room. Obviously, this involved technical difficulties.

Lady Churchill had foreseen that this might happen.
She bought a luggage elevator and had it fitted in the
dining room, thus avoiding any structural alteration. But
even this was not one hundred percent successful. On days
when we saw the Churchillian lower lip jutting out, we

knew that he was not only going to insist on walking from his bedroom to the drawing room, but that he intended ignoring the elevator and using the slippery winding staircase down to the dining room. It was rather difficult to know whose instructions to follow. Sir Winston would say, "Don't help me" as he doggedly set off from his bedroom. And Lady Churchill would tell us, "Make sure you hold his arm."

Whenever I tried to do this, he used to roar at me, even when guests were about: "Goddammit, man! Let go of me!"

Lady Churchill would intervene, saying, "Darling, he's only trying to help you."

This would quiet him a little, but he would still insist on walking alone.

"Oh, do let me be," he used to mutter, shrugging off any proffered assistance.

We knew that Lady Churchill was right but, at the same time, following her instructions meant incurring her husband's wrath. One just had to use one's common sense. After a while he became used to traveling up and down in the elevator and actually rather enjoyed it. Baroness Asquith, formerly Lady Violet Bonham Carter, a very old friend, used to accompany him in the elevator whenever she came for a meal. She had not been well and found the stairs rather exhausting.

There are people who, having suffered a physical handicap, make light of it, often joking about the problems it gives them. Sir Winston never joked about his broken leg. He seemed to take the view that such a handicap should be overcome as quickly as possible and could see nothing humorous in it.

The film shows that had been a feature of his stay in the Middlesex were continued once he returned to his London home. He was encouraged to have dinner in bed for the first few weeks, and the films were shown in his bedroom immediately after his tray had been cleared away.

Two men from the company that had supplied the films at the hospital would arrive at the house twice a week at about nine o'clock. One of them busied himself erecting a screen in front of the built-in dressing table directly opposite Sir Winston's bed. The other set up the projector on a bedside table, standing the sound amplifier at the side of the screen.

They usually brought along two feature films for Sir Winston to choose from. His secretaries still typed out a brief résumé of the plots to help him decide.

Before the lights were turned out, Lady Churchill would slip into the bedroom and settle down in an armchair to watch with her husband. The duty nurse was a third member of the bedroom audience, and sometimes the butler was invited in. Sir Winston preferred watching films to television, and I think this was mainly because the film screen was bigger and the pictures always in color. It was only in the last year of his life that he really turned to watching television.

He was, however, always keen to watch television when he had a horse running or when a big race was being shown. He seldom showed any signs of excitement watching a race on television but if one of his horses won then he would beam with pleasure.

The two men who brought the films always had a drink with him before the show started and sometimes he offered them a cigar. He really appreciated their coming, and as they left would shake them by the hand and thank them.

As he grew stronger and was able to get up for dinner, and a visit to Chartwell seemed within reach again, the film shows ceased. They did a tremendous amount of good during this stage of his convalescence.

About this time Sir Winston heard that Mr. Henry Baddeley, who had been his aide at the Battle of Omdurman in 1898, was celebrating his ninetieth birthday at his home at Prestwood, Buckinghamshire. He made a point of writing him a letter offering his good wishes "and remembrances of the famous battle." Mr. Baddeley had the letter framed and proudly hung it beside the saber he carried in the charge against the Dervishes. He recalled that this young subaltern in the 21st Lancers had first taught him how to make coffee.

Sir Winston's letters were always dictated to his secretary. Only when he wrote to Lady Churchill, members of the family, or very close personal friends, did he write in his own hand.

As I have said, his spirits were very high once he felt he was on the way to recovering from his broken leg. Each day that passed brought a gradual improvement in his walking, until he could manage to get about the house relying only on his stick.

Of course there were days when, because of a cold or other minor illness, he had to stay in bed. Whenever this happened his secretary typed out a short note on a slip of paper that was always headed, "Sir Winston," and neatly signed with the secretary's initials and the date.

The wording of the note would be couched very correctly. A typical message would read something like this: "I have confirmed that your doctors urged you most strongly not to attempt to come downstairs at present: it would certainly set back your recovery severely. Lady Churchill will come up and see you as soon as she feels a little better."

These notes helped us enormously and were often necessary because Sir Winston would claim that the doctors had given permission for him to get up when, in fact, they had not gone quite that far. The secretary then had the job of checking with the doctors to make quite sure of their instructions. The most diplomatic way he could put them to Sir Winston was in a polite note. Once handed the note, Sir Winston always read it and the message could not possibly then be misinterpreted.

Even so, Sir Winston would sometimes try to hoodwink us. "I'm getting up for lunch," he would say, hoping I had not seen the note. Quite firmly I would reply, "Sir Winston, I have read Mr. Montague Browne's note." He would then remain in bed.

One of the things that cheered him enormously was his completion of sixty years in politics. This anniversary he celebrated in October 1962, and it is worthwhile recalling that he was first elected to Parliament in 1900. He was returned as member for Oldham with a 222-vote majority, and the sixty years' total was reached because he was out of politics for two years when Dundee rejected him in 1922.

His statue at Woodford Green on the edge of Epping Forest was floodlit to celebrate the occasion. He sat for Woodford from 1945 until 1964. The anniversary was also marked by a special visit from Mr. Macmillan, then Prime Minister, who called for lunch, together with Lord Mountbatten, Chief of the Defense Staff.

The following month Sir Winston proved that he was fully recovered. He announced that he was going to have a night out, his first since his accident.

He arrived at the Savoy in grand style for a dinner of the Other Club, where he met a host of old friends.

He took the chairman's seat at the center of the U-shaped table group, and the chef made a point of including in the menu all Sir Winston's favorite dishes. The dinner's first course that night was Petite Marmite Savoy, the soup that was sent to him from the hotel's kitchens when he was in hospital. It was followed by fried fillet of sole wrapped in smoked salmon and garnished with scampi. Then came fillet of roast deer stuffed with *pâté de foie gras* and served, to Sir Winston's delight, with truffle sauce. It was indeed a dinner fit for a hero.

After serving coffee and brandy, the waiters withdrew and the doors of the Pinafore Room were closed. I was told later that Sir Winston gave an excellent off-the-cuff speech, which had been warmly received.

It looked as if he was going to stay there talking all night because most of the guests had left when he finally decided to make a move shortly before midnight. He even outstayed the Prime Minister.

It was a damp night, but Sir Winston, well muffled against the cold, cheerfully raised his black homburg and waved his cigar as he left. He insisted on walking to his car, and it was obvious that, as far as he was concerned, he was fully recovered. He proved it by returning to the hotel the next month for another of the club's dinners. This time the worst smog of the year swirled round the Savoy and quite a few members decided that conditions were too bad for them to attend; but not the founder member.

With his black hat set at a rakish angle, the honorable member for Woodford announced to his household, "Of course I must go." There were some doubtful looks but he had his way as usual and he determinedly climbed into his car, which gradually groped its way through the smog to the Savoy. He was so keen to be present that he was the second member to arrive! Only eleven members of the club attended that night. It really was a most remarkable recovery.

More than ever before Sir Winston now looked forward to one of his favorite pastimes: playing cards. He had always played, both when at home and on vacation, but he seemed to play more often in the last years. The cards came out most afternoons and practically every evening after dinner, and invariably the game was bezique. Lady Churchill and some close friends and relations like her cousin, the Hon. Sylvia Henley, Mrs. Lady Juliet Duff, or Baroness Asquith, would often play with him for an hour or so in the afternoon.

Mrs. Henley, upright and sprightly, had a shrill, penetrating voice and a fondness for red hats. She was elderly, devoted a great deal of her time to charitable works, and still drove her own car.

Lady Juliet Duff was tall and elegant with the grace one usually associates with a princess. She was as soft-spoken as Mrs. Henley was loud-voiced.

The third bezique enthusiast, Baroness Asquith, was a great admirer of Sir Winston. She was an extremely clever woman with a slight stoop and could always be relied upon to spice the conversation over cards with her own charming witticisms.

All three ladies were welcome visitors who did much to entertain Sir Winston, especially during afternoons when he might otherwise have been rather lonely.

Lord Montgomery used to play whenever he was staying at Chartwell. I remember one crack he made when, as usual, I was called in to shuffle the cards. He watched me for some time as I fluttered the cards from hand to hand and then said, in that rasping voice of his, "The way you do that, young man, indicates a misspent youth."

For once I was able to come back with the right answer. "Actually sir," I replied, "I leaned to shuffle cards this way through playing poker in the army." Montgomery thought this a huge joke.

There were about two hundred packs of playing cards in the drawing-room cupboard at Chartwell, all of them sent in batches from America. They were gifts from an admirer who had them specially printed. Each card had, on its back, Sir Winston's signature printed in black against a white backing. The packs of cards, edged with either red or blue, were broken open about once every two months. A dozen boxes of cards used to be kept in London and whenever Sir Winston went abroad twelve packs always went with him.

Mr. Montague Browne sometimes played with Sir Winston if Lady Churchill was out shopping in the afternoon. He knew that Sir Winston was a very good player and the two men spent many hours quietly enjoying their game in the drawing room. They used to play for small stakes but in the last year or so this stopped.

There was never any question of Sir Winston not playing bezique after dinner, nor did any one ever mention the game. The cards were automatically set out on the small green baize-topped table in the corner near the window. It was all part of the regular ritual.

XII

The Household

S<small>IR</small> W<small>INSTON</small> was at the center of quite a small organization in his two homes. Some description of these may be interesting.

Mr. Anthony Montague Browne, his private secretary, had stayed on at his side after serving him at Number Ten, Downing Street. A conscientious and very efficient man, he took the important private letters in to Sir Winston every morning, and then, if a reply was needed, would call for one of the girl secretaries to come and take dictation.

He worked from an office that, after Sir Winston's discharge from the Middlesex Hospital, was converted into Sir Winston's bedroom. When this happened he moved into a small office that had a bathroom leading off it. It was formerly a secretary's bedroom.

Every afternoon he drove to the Foreign Office to collect various documents that required Sir Winston's attention. On his return he sometimes joined in a game of cards or made arrangements for Sir Winston's social life. He was constantly kept busy organizing and acting as a go-between.

Mr. Montague Browne also acted as press officer, taking all newspaper enquiries and generally indicating to his superior when it might be advisable to make statements. This in itself was a considerable responsibility, as newspapers were constantly ringing up with a variety of queries.

He naturally traveled everywhere with Sir Winston, sometimes taking his wife with him on the cruises. He had thinning brown hair and thin features; a very well-read man, he was rather fond of quoting from books he had recently read.

But although he was at the center of things, the real hub of the household both in London and Chartwell was always a gray-haired, smartly-dressed precise woman, Miss Grace Hamblin.

Miss Hamblin was Lady Churchill's secretary, companion, and close friend. She had been awarded the O.B.E. after the war for her work at Number Ten and was a very loyal and tireless servant.

Apart from looking after all Lady Churchill's affairs, she ran both houses, interviewed staff, arranged their salaries, organized the kitchens, even did the shopping. When Lady Churchill wanted to go out for a walk in the park, Miss Hamblin would be at her side; when Lady Churchill was ill in hospital, she visited her every day. She even found time to arrange all the flowers in the house, and was generally liked by everyone on the staff.

When we were down at Chartwell, Mr. Montague Browne used to commute daily from his London flat. But Miss Hamblin stayed down in the country at her cottage in the grounds of Chartwell. She never obtruded in any way, always being able to make both visitors and servants feel at ease with her pleasant personality.

Two women dealt with Sir Winston's personal mail. They worked in a large office just off Mr. Montague Browne's and were reinforced by other secretaries whenever there was a special occasion. The two were Miss Doreen Pugh, a short, rather petite brunette, and Miss

Catherine Snelling, younger and taller, with light brown, shoulder-length hair.

One came on duty at nine o'clock every morning, finishing at five; the other arrived at eleven, working through until half past seven in the evening. Their many duties included arranging all trips abroad, going to great lengths to ensure that Sir Winston wore the correct dress and medals for social events, acting as secretaries to Mr. Montague Browne, taking all incoming telephone calls, organizing the frequent film shows, calling in person at the public libraries to choose books for Sir Winston, and carrying them back by car.

Most of these books were well thumbed and were often ones that he had read before. If he considered a book good, he would ask to read it again and sometimes read the same book as many as three times in a year.

The secretaries knew that he liked autobiographies and that among his favorite authors were Somerset Maugham, Rudyard Kipling, Sir Walter Scott, and Robert Louis Stevenson. He sometimes read books that he himself had written. I do not remember him ever reading mysteries or detective stories, at least not modern ones, although he did read *Witness for the Prosecution* after seeing the film.

Lady Churchill selects her own books from Harrods. She buys books frequently and, like her husband, enjoys autobiographies, making a point of reading all those in the list of bestsellers. She also reads a lot of romantic novels, particularly those by Barbara Cartland, mother of the Countess of Dartmouth, formerly Lady Lewisham. Occasionally Lady Churchill tackles an historical novel in French, and things like *Dr. Zhivago,* but on the whole she tends to favor light reading.

Sir Winston usually borrowed about a dozen books at a time from the public library at either Kensington or Westerham, and when we were on the Riviera, besides taking library books out there with him, he used the "British Library" in Monte Carlo.

He disliked books with small print, preferring ones he could read with a minimum of effort. There were times when he read nine of the twelve the secretaries took, but six out of twelve was the usual score.

The books were always taken to Sir Winston when he was resting in bed during the early evening. The secretary would sit at his bedside and hand over the selection for him to examine. He would then skim through them, returning any that did not take his fancy.

If he had finished his current library book, he selected one from the new batch for immediate reading. He placed the others in a pile on his small table.

Most of his reading was done either in bed or in the drawing room, and after reaching the end of a book he would hand it to me saying, "I don't want to see *his* face again!" He often referred to objects as "he."

The two secretaries visited the public library every two weeks, and if books became overdue, the fines were paid out of petty cash. Although Sir Winston was presented with many books, gifts from his family, friends, and sometimes authors, he continued to borrow from the public libraries; and the secretaries, who were used to his literary tastes, were rarely far wrong in their selection.

A rather unusual social scale existed within the household. It was never more apparent than when a new nurse arrived. Instead of neatly fitting in and being friends with everyone, she would find herself resented by the domestic staff and looked down upon by the secretarial staff. The nurses had, perhaps, the toughest job of all. They were the watchdogs, hired to ensure that Sir Winston was kept in continual good health. It was not easy. So many people wanted to help. And everyone constantly offered advice on what should or should not be done.

Two of Sir Winston's favorite nurses were Glenda Mc-Alpin, the cigar-smoking Australian, and Ann Huddleston, a tall girl from Yorkshire.

Nurse McAlpin trained at the Royal Melbourne Hospital and was picked by Lady Churchill from a short list soon after she arrived in London in 1961. Off duty she enjoyed skiing, golf, and speeding in her white sports car.

She played a big part in Sir Winston's recovery from his broken leg, and he held her in very high regard. When her mother and aunt came to Europe for a tour, they stopped off at Monte Carlo where Sir Winston met them at his hotel.

Both nurses were in their twenties. Ann Huddleston replaced Nurse McAlpin when she decided to visit Switzerland a year before Sir Winston's death.

Miss Huddleston had a quiet, unassuming manner, firm but very gentle when dealing with Sir Winston. She was a girl who could make even a nurse's uniform look glamorous, and with the kind of smile that lights up a face and suddenly makes it beautiful.

She loved Sir Winston very much, as we all did in our own individual ways. When he died she wept as if she had lost a very close relative.

Whenever she accompanied him into the drawing room to meet his guests, she never obtruded as some of the nurses were apt to do by speaking in a loud voice as if to assert themselves. Miss Huddleston would fade into the background in such a way that the guests never really noticed that she was there. She was aware of Sir Winston's greatness but never lost her sense of proportion.

The butler, Enrique, was a Spaniard. He took over in 1964 from a young, dynamic Swiss boy, Walter, who was a most impressive character. Walter arrived in England unable to speak a word of the language and had never held a butler's post before. His aunt was working in the household as a lady's maid and she recommended him to Lady Churchill.

He was hired as a parlor man and soon proved his worth. He had a cool, aloof manner and plenty of confidence. And he became butler in less than a year. He obviously had no intention of making a career out of the promotion, and made it clear that he planned to become a caterer and open a restaurant. Sir Winston immediately took to him because Walter could anticipate everything he wanted.

Enrique, on the other hand, was also popular. He was an older man who made no close friends among the staff but was nevertheless well liked. On his day off he attended afternoon classes to improve his English. He was a rather serious man who seldom joked and went about his work with methodical efficiency.

He could be moody and was at times very nervous, with a habit of walking up and down when he had a problem on his mind. He was the typical Spaniard with dark hair and dark brown eyes, but an extremely hard worker who worried over the smallest details of his job.

The household ran four relatively modest cars: a black Humber Pullman, used only for Sir Winston and Lady Churchill; a dark blue Humber Super Snipe estate car, for shuttling luggage between London and Chartwell; a gray Hillman Husky, for carrying such things as parcels, groceries and logs; and a blue Morris Oxford, which was Lady Churchill's own car.

The man who drove all these was Mr. Joe Bullock. He was not on the payroll in later years because he worked for the Rootes group as a chauffeur and demonstrator. He was, however, made available for Sir Winston, being generally regarded as his personal driver.

Bullock was a big man with broad shoulders, devoted to Sir Winston and first-class at his job. Whenever he drove Lady Churchill it was at a steady 30 m.p.h. But when her husband was by himself in the back seat, he used to encourage Bullock to go faster, tapping on the glass partition and calling out, "GO ON!" Whenever he felt Bullock was slow in overtaking he would lean forward and bellow, "NOW!" As in everything else Sir Winston had a constant sense of urgency. It does Bullock great credit that he never really took the chances his passenger would have liked him to take.

Lady Churchill often accompanied her husband on drives up to town, and when this happened Bullock really was in an impossible position. Murray, the detective, would sit at his side, quietly murmuring, "Slow down here," or, "Pull in to the left a little more." And in the back Sir Winston would be glowering because he felt they should be traveling faster. Bullock, conscious that he was also driving Lady Churchill, was always afraid to put his foot down.

Bullock usually stayed in London unless the Humber was required at Chartwell. His opposite number at Sir Winston's country home was Mr. Joe Jenner, who ran his own rental-car business in Westerham. Jenner was a big man like Bullock; friendly, very generous and always willing to stop and chat about his experiences with Sir Winston "in the old days."

He had driven Sir Winston off and on ever since he first bought his country home and, in later years, spent much of his time chauffering visitors between the house and the railway station. Several people used to drive the Super Snipe and the Husky when these chauffeurs were not available. Miss Hamblin drove Lady Churchill's car.

The rest of the staff consisted of an Italian lady's maid, two housemaids, a kitchenmaid, a daily woman, and a Scots cook. Four gardeners worked at Chartwell, sending up potted plants and flowers to decorate the London home. The head gardener was Mr. Victor Vincent, who had been with the family seventeen years. He was an extremely experienced man, rather independent in his manner but always cheerful and fond of trotting out an occasional joke. His accent, a rural Kentish drawl, was a delight to the ear.

One of his special prides was the melons he cultivated in the oil-heated glasshouses on the south slopes of the walled garden. They were true hot-house melons of the Blenheim Orange variety, a rather rare delicacy because few gardeners know how to look after them. The melons, however, were the cause of Mr. Vincent being involved in a rather unfortunate experience that for a time upset his employers.

It happened this way. A Sunday newspaper, anxious for some gossip items about Sir Winston, discovered that Mr. Vincent was the head gardener at Chartwell. They telephoned Miss Hamblin and asked her if they could interview him. She referred them to Mr. Montague Browne, who politely told them that he thought such an interview would be unwise.

The newspaper was not deterred. The reporter assigned to the story went down to Chartwell and told Mr. Vincent, "We've spoken to Mr. Montague Browne and want to ask you a few questions about your job." He omitted to say that although he had spoken to Sir Winston's secretary, he had been told not to approach him. Mr. Vincent, believing that the secretary had approved, talked to the reporter and the piece duly appeared in the newspaper's gossip column. Naturally Mr. Vincent was in trouble over the incident, an example of how certain newspapers can sometimes cut corners to get the information they require.

It reminds me of the time one of Madame Floris' huge iced birthday cakes was being delivered at Chartwell for Sir Winston. A huge crowd had gathered round the gates, and when the Floris' truck arrived the cake was carried into the dining room. What the family did not know was that one of the men carrying the cake was a reporter who had somehow inveigled himself into helping with the delivery.

Lady Churchill always made a point of shaking hands with the delivery men to thank them for their trouble, and when she shook this particular fellow's hand she was rather taken aback when he revealed himself as a reporter and started asking her questions about the birthday celebrations! The poor man was shown out straight away, but everyone had to admire his ingenuity and cool nerve.

At least he was attempting to get his facts right. On many occasions we were amused at some of the garbled stories that seemed to get into print, garbled no doubt because little information about Sir Winston was ever given to the press during the last seven years of his life. There was a story printed in an American magazine that Lady Churchill always had sweet-smelling incense burning in the hall at Hyde Park Gate. The author went on to describe further details of the house, all, like the incense, products of an extremely lively imagination.

It is fair to say that everyone who worked in the household was devoted to the great man. Without any effort on his part, he commanded complete loyalty and respect. This was nothing at all to do with the legend of Sir Winston; it was something that stemmed from his authority. People on the outside often saw him as an image rather than the mortal being he was. Working as close to him as we were, the image faded, and one was always conscious of the man himself, his great strength, both physical and mental, and his overwhelming personality.

XIII

"Pass me the scissors"

ONE morning when Sir Winston was in bed reading one of his own early books, he put it down on the counterpane and said to me, "Have you read this?" I told him that I had not.

Without batting an eyelid he replied, "You should. It's awfully well written, you know."

It was a typical example of his "deadpan" humor. He was very fond of dry witticisms. But he could take a joke as well. Once, when we were in Monte Carlo, I went to collect him in the dining room after lunch, and he frowned because I was wearing a gray sport shirt and gray flannels.

"I don't very much like your garb," he said.

I replied, "Well, Sir Winston, if you will buy me a Riviera suit I would be glad to wear it." His eyes twinkled and he did not take offense. "Ho! Ho!" he chuckled, and said nothing further about my clothes. He did not buy me the suit.

There were times when one was rather baffled by some of his remarks, not knowing if he were joking or not. A perfect example of this was when he mysteriously called back one of his nurses just as she was leaving the house.

She had rather lovely legs, and Sir Winston told her in conspiratorial tones, "Uh-huh ... my dear ... you've got *very* pretty legs. If you are going home now, you had better ask the policeman to escort you across the park, because they have wind of the fact that I have a nurse with pretty legs."

We never discovered who "they" were, and even to this day I am not sure if this was another example of his dry humor.

Sir Winston was, on the whole, very concerned about the welfare of his staff, particularly when he was vacationing abroad. Shortly after arriving at his hotel, he would ask them, "Did you have a good meal? Is everything all right?" On one occasion when I was going off duty he asked, "Where are you off to tonight?" I told him that I was thinking of going to the Casino. "If you go there you will want some money," he said. He was obviously prepared to give me some, but I declined.

He sometimes lost his temper, but I never heard him swear outside the privacy of his bedroom. And then he would swear mainly to see if he could shock me. His most common expression was "Goddammit!" But he could use short Anglo-Saxon words, particularly when he was really roused and there was no one about.

Each time he did this he would give me a sidelong glance with the hint of a smile, as if to say, "I suppose you don't approve." I did approve. It showed that he was, after all, very human.

I remember one morning when he was smoking a giant cigar in bed and reading a book, he accidentally burned a hole in the sheet. It was not the first time that it had happened, and he had already been told off about it by Lady Churchill. He looked down and saw that the cigar had made a hole about the size of half a crown.

"Pass me the scissors!" he said calmly.

He then proceeded to cut out the burn marks, leaving an even larger hole. It was rather like a mischievous little schoolboy trying to cover up his misdemeanors.

To ensure that he did not continue to ruin the sheets with cigar burns, some colored linen napkins were bought. They were laid out across the top of the sheets, but even this maneuver was not entirely successful.

I was outside his bedroom one morning when I heard him shouting, and rushed in to find the room full of smoke. He had set fire to one of the napkins and flung it over the side of the bed. It had landed on the carpet, burned a hole, and set fire to the bed's flounce.

After extinguishing the fire, I told him, "Sir Winston, you really should be more careful. You could have burned to death."

He carried on puffing on his cigar and replied calmly, "Oh no. I would have . . . uh . . . leaped out."

The thought of him leaping out of bed at his age may seem remarkable, but I am quite sure that he would have done it. He was completely unruffled by the incident and did not worry about a large piece of yellow carpet that had to be renewed and the bed flounce repaired.

He strenuously resisted all attempts to stop him from smoking in bed, but from that day on he was never left alone when it was clear that he intended doing this. It was, however, virtually impossible to separate him from his cigars. He smoked them in the bath, when he was dressing, even when using his electric razor.

He would seldom knock the ash from a cigar, and consequently it would then fall onto a clean shirt front. As he never allowed any spare time when changing clothes, this habit of his made life very difficult for me.

I would say, "You can't go out looking like that, Sir Winston. I'll get the clothes brush."

126

His answer was to rub the cigar ash deeper into his suit saying, "Oh, it's all right. Stop worrying, man."

Firmly brushing the suit, I used to do my best to tidy him up, but it was always a running battle with him interjecting, "Oh, *do* stop," and "I *must* go."

When I told him that it would reflect on me if he went out looking untidy, I knew the answer I would get.

"Nonsense," he muttered.

All the time I was trying to brush him down he would be moving toward the front door. There was never any question of his standing still to be brushed.

If the marks were not too prominent we got away with it by brushing them over with dusting powder. But if they were rather noticeable, the shirt had to come off and tempers began to fray all round.

At the end of his life, when he gave up shaving himself, the nurses took it in turns and one would see them doing their difficult job through a dense smoke screen.

April 1963 was a month that stands out in my memory. In the first place it was the month he returned to the Riviera to complete the holiday interrupted when he broke his leg. It was also the month in which he completed fifty years as the oldest serving brother of the Elder Brethren of Trinity House and became the oldest British Prime Minister ever to have lived. He was also made an honorary citizen of the United States, as well as a full-fledged member of the National Congress of American Indians!

It was typical of the man that at the first possible opportunity he chose to return to the south of France, as if to prove that he was fully recovered again. He had an extraordinary reception when he arrived at Nice Airport and a special escort of police motorcycle riders when he drove to his hotel in Monte Carlo.

A few days before he set off on his holiday, he sat in an

armchair at his London home to watch a live TV broadcast of the Washington ceremony at which President Kennedy made him an honorary citizen of the United States. He was extremely annoyed that he was not able to go to America for the actual ceremony, but had the satisfaction of seeing his son Randolph and grandson Winston stand in for him.

He saw the program after quietly dining with Lady Churchill, and was impressed that it was relayed direct by an American communications space satellite. The next day he had a visit from the American Ambassador who handed him his U.S. passport.

He had a very strong affection for the Americans, and I believe he made at least sixteen visits to the United States, frequently to speak on notable occasions.

The day after he had started his holiday on the Riviera he achieved another remarkable distinction. He became the most long-lived British Prime Minister, beating the record for longevity held by Mr. Gladstone, who was over eighty-eight when he died in 1898.

Most of the congratulatory telegrams were delivered to his London home, but they were sent on to Sir Winston on the Riviera. He celebrated the day sunning himself on the balcony of his eighth-floor suite overlooking the harbor, lunching with M. Jean-Pierre Moatti, Prefect of the Alpes Maritimes, and his wife, and then embarking on a two-hour tour of the hills beyond Monaco.

It was about this time that Sir Winston became a Red Indian. He had been invited some months earlier by the National Congress of American Indians to join their ranks. They pointed out that he was a direct descendant of the Iroquois tribe through his mother Mrs. Jennie Jerome Churchill. Sir Winston, thrilled at this, accepted the membership invitation, thus notching up yet another unusual achievement.

He completed fifty years as one of the Elder Brethren of Trinity House at the end of the month. These are the men who carry on the centuries-old job of organizing the pilots and navigational lights that guide shipping vessels round Britain. One of his favorite uniforms was the smart navy blue of an Elder Brother, and he particularly liked the peaked naval cap that went with it.

This brings me to his love of hats. At some time or other he must have been photographed in every conceivable kind, ranging from American Stetsons to Russian Astrakhans. Many of these were stacked in hat boxes in a special cupboard outside Lady Churchill's bedroom. There were military hats, naval hats, a white pith helmet, an Australian bush hat, and countless others.

He had six broad-brimmed Stetsons, four gray and two white, all kept above the wardrobe in his bedroom. With them were piled two black Homburgs, two gray Homburgs, a Panama hat given him by Margot Fonteyn, two black top hats, and a gray one. After he became a member of the Congress of American Indians, the full regalia of a North American Indian chieftain, which had actually been worn during the frontier wars, was delivered to Chartwell. The tunic was decorated with the scalps of enemies killed in battle and the trousers, made of buffalo hide, were marked with blood stains. The huge feathered war headdress was very heavy and decorated round the band with colored beads.

Someone once said that Sir Winston was the only man in London who owned more hats than his wife. He was right. Lady Churchill rarely wore a hat. Her husband thoroughly enjoyed discovering new headgear, and he had a tremendous flair for looking exactly right no matter what he put on his head. Most of the photographs of Sir Winston outdoors prove this, from the hussar helmet he wore as a subaltern in 1896 to the huge beplumed hat he wore as a Knight of the Garter.

Sir Winston was adamant about wearing the right hat for the right occasion. On vacation he would have a variety of hats but always there was a Stetson near at hand. It was the type of hat he seemed to like most. He would take all six whenever he went abroad and there were often as many as eight hat boxes among his luggage.

Sir Winston decided that May that he would not stand for Parliament at the next general election. He wrote to the chairman of his divisional Conservative Association in Woodford that his accident had made it difficult for him to take his place in the House as often as he would wish. He notified them well in advance because he wanted to give his successor time to make himself known in the constituency.

He wrote in his letter, "I need not tell you with what sadness I feel constrained to take this step. I have now had the honor and privilege of sitting in the House of Commons for more than sixty years; for thirty-nine of these I have represented Epping and then Woodford. It is against the background of the unswerving support of the people of southwest Essex that the most important phases of my political life have unfolded. I shall never forget your loyalty and kindness to my wife and myself over these momentous years."

The night that he made the announcement, he attended the Royal Academy's dinner, rather depressed at the decision he had just taken. However, he had his usual talk about painting and painters with his old friend Sir Charles Wheeler, the Academy's President. He also ran over the political scene with Mr. Butler and Earl Attlee, but his longest conversation was with Lord Montgomery, who sat beside him.

Lord Montgomery tried to cheer him up, leaning forward on his chair and nodding his head as he emphasized certain points. Sir Winston, wearing his blue ribbon of the Garter and the medallion of the Order of Merit round his neck, sat staring into space. The Commons was the spur to his life and giving up his seat was a tremendous turning point in his career. That night for the first time in his life he did not tour the galleries to see the pictures, returning straight home after the dinner. Despite the occasion and the company, it was a sad night for Sir Winston.

A lot of people suggested that he should be made an honorary member of the House of Commons, and for a time there even seemed to be a chance that this might happen. Some were against it; in particular, Earl Attlee, who said he had never heard a more preposterous proposal. He pointed out that if a distinguished statesman wanted to continue as a legislator there was always the House of Lords.

"The House of Commons," he said, "is not a club but a legislative body composed entirely of members elected by, and responsible to, a constituency." He added that he could not believe Sir Winston would ever approve such a proposal, which would weaken the elected basis of the House, even though it were done merely to do him honor.

From Sir Winston there was only a dignified silence. He never canvassed honors and probably no one will ever know how he really felt about this.

Two weeks later, however, he showed that although he intended giving up his seat at the general election, he would carry on attending the Chamber until then. He drove to the Commons. Slowly, and with great courage, the old warrior made his way to his seat, frailty somewhat emphasized by the size of his son-in-law, Mr. Christopher Soames, who held his arm. Everyone agreed that the standing ovation he received was the kind that Prime Ministers get after winning a general election.

It was his first visit since a few days before breaking his leg, and the House was pretty full, word having got round that he was on his way. His favorite seat at the corner of the Front Bench just below the gangway had been kept by the Tory M.P. for Watford, who, as soon as he saw Sir Winston moving toward him, bowed and offered it to him. The greatest Commoner settled down as if he had never been away, smiling when Mr. Macmillan welcomed him back as "our most distinguished member."

XIV

Lady Churchill

M UCH has been written and much more probably
will be written about Lady Churchill, that great lady who
was in her eightieth year when her husband died. She has
so many exceptional qualities: dignity, charm, strength,
patience, all of these and many more besides.

But the public never saw the real woman behind the
man. Sir Winston always called her "Clemmie," yet she
never abbreviated his name, always calling him "Winston"
when in the company of relatives and friends and "Sir
Winston" when with anyone outside this tight circle.

She was self-effacing to a degree, stepping out of the lime-
light whenever it was on her husband. And it was on him
the best part of his life.

Of her he once said, "My marriage was much the most
fortunate and joyous event which happened to me in the
whole of my life, for what can be more glorious than to be
united in one's walk in life with a being incapable of an
ignoble thought?"

Perhaps her daughter, Mrs. Mary Soames, will have the
last word when she finishes her mother's biography, but I

can describe how I found her during those last years of her husband's life.

Her greatest quality was undoubtedly her strength of character and the fact that she could temper this with graciousness. Whenever a crisis loomed, she was able to meet it, never wavering at her husband's side. The unselfish devotion and encouragement she gave him cannot be overestimated. She was the strong woman behind the strong man.

She did not tolerate inefficiency, nor did she ever spare herself. Once when she was ill in bed and running a high temperature, guests were due for an important luncheon. She got up an hour before they arrived to make sure her instructions had been thoroughly carried out.

She is immensely practical and businesslike. Some years before I joined Sir Winston, they sat down to lunch one Sunday and a goose was placed for him to carve. He was about to do this when he suddenly remembered something and pushed the dish away.

"You carve, Clemmie," he said. "He was a friend of mine."

The fact that the goose had also been a friend of Lady Churchill's made no difference. She took the carving knife and fork from her husband and dealt with the bird as if to say, "Sentiment is all very well but let's get on with the lunch."

She had acted as hostess to practically all the eminent men and women of her time. Even in the last years of her husband's life she still had a fairly heavy list of social engagements. Visitors who came for lunch or dinner usually found themselves offered good English dishes such as clear soup, fresh trout or sole, roast beef or a plump pheasant, sweets and cheeses. Occasionally she slipped in a savory dish after picking up the recipe in a woman's magazine.

If Sir Winston was not feeling up to holding a lengthy

conversation with his visitors, his wife invariably kept the conversation flowing in her charming unaffected way. No one who visited her home ever felt ill at ease when she was there.

She never deliberately courted publicity. If the photographers were waiting outside the house to take pictures, she sometimes tried to step out of the way. When they asked her to stay at his side, she always appeared genuinely flattered that they should want the two of them together.

Lady Churchill, with her beautifully kept white hair and lasting good looks, always held herself very erect. She had been a first-class tennis player and, indeed, is very well informed about the game. She attended Wimbledon most years, sometimes sitting in the Royal Box with Princess Marina, and always makes a point of attending the Women's Final. The year Christine Truman reached the final, Lady Churchill sent a telegram of encouragement; Miss Truman comes from Sir Winston's constituency.

Whenever she has the opportunity, Lady Churchill keeps fit by taking long walks, something she particularly enjoys. Like all her family, she loves French films, old music-hall songs, American magazines, and visiting the theatre. She always enjoyed meeting people connected with the theatre to keep up to date on shows in the West End.

Her voice is fine and clear, and she still diets to keep her slim figure. She was an expert in smoothing over awkward moments with her husband and certainly had plenty of practice. After all, she had fifty-six years experience of the full range of Churchillian moods.

Every morning she was awake at 7:30 A.M., taking her breakfast in bed at 8 A.M. and, like her husband, reading all the papers right through.

At 9 A.M. she would see the cook to check over the day's menus, which were always planned a week in advance.

Then the butler would take the mail up to her and receive his instructions for the day.

The next person to see her was always Miss Hamblin. Lady Churchill dictated letters, reviewed the various appointments of the day, and straightened out minor problems. She ran both households down to the last detail. Her organizing abilities were tremendous. For instance, Sir Winston always had champagne with his meals, but she knew some of their guests preferred other wines and she went out of her way to see that they had them.

As soon as Sir Winston was awake, she would go to his room, give him a morning kiss, and tell him which guests were calling during the day. She then organized flowers for his room and toured the house to supervise the floral arrangements.

She had a small tiled balcony outside her first-floor sitting room and always had it filled with plants. One of her great loves was gardening, and at Chartwell she would spend hours going round the gardens in cotton gloves pruning the roses.

She usually kept away from the kitchens, being a wise enough woman to leave the actual preparation of meals to her excellent cook.

Once a week the hairdresser and manicurist called, and some days, when she felt in the mood, she would take herself off shopping, accompanied by her secretary, who drove the car. Like other shoppers, they frequently found difficulty in parking the Morris Oxford, but she never expected preferential treatment, driving round and round the streets until a parking meter was found.

At 12:45 P.M. she would be back at Hyde Park Gate receiving her guests, entertaining them in the drawing room with cocktails while they waited for Sir Winston to join them. Sometimes she left them for a few minutes to slip out to make sure her husband was going to be ready in time. This was always a problem for her, because unpunctuality at mealtimes was one of his big weaknesses. Yet she invariably managed to get round this difficulty with her charm and tact.

She went to great pains to make sure that the seating arrangements were right and always put herself opposite her husband. She rang for each course by pushing a small portable buzzer that was connected directly to the pantry. After coffee, taken at the dining table, the ladies retired to the drawing room while the men drank their brandies and smoked their cigars.

Lunch was always served at 1:15 P.M. and was usually over by 2:30 P.M. If Sir Winston was going to the House of Commons he left at 2:40 P.M., and this timetable was rigidly adhered to. Lady Churchill would go upstairs to her sitting room to write letters or read a book. If Sir Winston was staying indoors, the cards were automatically put out, and Lady Churchill would spend an hour playing bezique with her husband. Later she would wrap a silk scarf round her head and set off with Miss Hamblin for a walk in Kensington Gardens. On her return she took tea in her sitting room, or, if a guest had arrived, in the drawing room. Sir Winston never drank tea but would join them at the table with a whisky and soda.

After the afternoon guests had left, Lady Churchill would go to her room, write more letters and then take her afternoon nap between 6:30 P.M. and 7:30 P.M. She was always down in the drawing room to greet her evening guests at 8 P.M., with dinner served at 8:15 P.M. This was the time Sir Winston liked to eat, but Lady Churchill really liked her meal earlier, and whenever he was away she would arrange for it to be served at half-past seven.

As I have said, it was extremely difficult to persuade Sir Winston to be ready for dinner on time, especially when he was reading in bed. He was invariably late and always blamed me when he discovered that his guests had been waiting for him some time. I used to remind him at least half an hour before dinner, but it was often wasted effort.

The conversation would go something like this:

"Sir Winston, it is a quarter to eight and dinner will be served in half an hour's time. Don't you think you ought to get ready?"

"I will just finish this page."

"Sir Winston, it is now eight o'clock and the guests will be arriving any minute. You really must make a move."

"I will just read to the end of this page."

Sometimes he did not even reply, he would be so deeply buried in his book. It was rather a strain, because I always felt that it was my responsibility to have Sir Winston at the dinner table on time. We did our best not to seek Lady Churchill's help too often.

It took him about a quarter of an hour to get dressed, twice as long if he had a bath. I had the schedule worked out to the last minute, but sometimes, just before he was about to leave for the drawing room, he would say, "I think I'll do my nails."

This threw the timetable right out.

Holding out a hand, he said, "Nail file."

I would hand him the nail file. Then he would hold his hand out again and say, "Clippers." Again I was expected to put them straight into the palm of his hand. It rather reminded me of a surgeon in the operating room.

It often appeared that the more one tried to rush Sir Winston, the slower he was determined to be. It was as if he knew of one's anxiety to have him ready in time.

I once told him, "This really is too bad. You're late *again,* Sir Winston."

His eyes twinkled and rather mischievously he gave a little smile and said, "Uh, uh, I'm not *always* late, Howes."

Dinner would be followed by cards in the drawing room

and then, after saying goodnight to her husband about ten, Lady Churchill would go to her room. She always listened to the ten o'clock B.B.C. newscast when she got into bed and was asleep half an hour to an hour later. If there were guests she stayed up an extra half an hour, but rarely went to bed later than half-past ten.

Lady Churchill decided on the decoration of every room in the house. None of them was wallpapered; they were all painted or distempered in pale tints.

At Christmas time she took on the enormous task of buying all the presents and sending out all the cards. The presents would be bought at the end of November, most of them delivered to the house after she had made her selection in the shops.

Their Christmas card was always a color reproduction of one of Sir Winston's paintings. Inside the card was printed, "With Christmas thoughts and wishes from Winston and Clementine Churchill." The people they sent them to ranged from the Queen to an ex-cook. Lady Churchill could remember all of her husband's paintings, and it was largely on her recommendation that the choice was made.

Some of the household staff used to get Christmas boxes, which came directly out of Sir Winston's racecourse winnings. The girl secretaries got things like a set of traveling cases, a charm bracelet, or items of jewelry. I always received cash and signed copies of Sir Winston's books.

Whenever he had a birthday, Lady Churchill was faced with the ticklish problem of what to do with some of the hundreds of presents that poured in from all over the world. It was obviously impossible for them to eat all the perishable goods that were delivered and, as discreetly as possible, she arranged for some of these to be sent to hospitals and charities.

She loved croquet and, whenever she was at Chartwell, spent hours playing, often in the morning and afternoon. The croquet lawn had been a tennis court but was converted when the children grew up.

She played mainly with Lady Birley, Mrs. Henley, Lord Montgomery, Baroness Asquith, and Mr. Montague Browne. Sometimes Sir Winston would appear on the scene at the end of a game and have a little practice on his own. He used to discard his walking stick, using the croquet mallet as a prop in between shots. He would line up a ball, steady himself, and get it through the hoop the first time. He was never mediocre at anything.

Most summer afternoons at Chartwell he spent watching his wife playing for an hour or so before taking himself off on a trip to the fishponds. All the time Lady Churchill would be keenly wrapped up in her game, and the click of the croquet balls and the penetrating voice of Lord Montgomery, often her partner, would echo across the lawns.

She rarely went outside the grounds and spent a lot of time with Mr. Vincent and his team of gardeners, showing a great interest in their greenhouse work. If the Soames children were visiting during the summer, she would take them all down to the swimming pool before tea. She did not swim at Chartwell, obviously preferring the warmer waters of the Mediterranean.

One of her great pleasures was to stand at the side of the pool and watch the youngsters happily splashing about. Another was to walk down to the big lake with the children's nanny to watch me row the children out to fish off the island. There was an abundance of fish and they were easy to catch.

She would enjoy the expedition as much as her grandchildren, roaring with laughter every time there was a wild shriek of, "Look what I've caught, grandmama!" Sometimes the children would trail back to the house with the fish they had caught for her, carefully wrapped in dock leaves. Never once was she too busy to enter into the spirit of things, always showing interest in the muddy tench and perch presented to her.

The fish were never eaten and had to be quietly disposed of after the children had gone. I never allowed one child to catch more than the others to avoid tears, and so they used to throw a lot of the fish back.

They were happy days. Lady Churchill, who had led a very active public life, and indeed was still very active socially, was never happier.

When Chartwell was open to the public, she would make an appearance with Sir Winston on the little terrace at the back of her bedroom. They would both wave to the visitors thronging the lawns. It was easy to see why they did not mingle with the crowds—they would have been mobbed.

During the summer she would entertain members of the Woodford Conservative Association for tea on the lawns. A team of caterers took over for the day, leaving her free to mingle with the constituents.

No matter how she was feeling she was always graciousness itself, spending a few minutes with everyone present. But there was never any question of her wishing to be the center of attraction.

In her late seventies, when most people would be wanting to take things quietly, she was as active as ever, backing up her husband with the same tireless devotion she had shown in all their long years of married life.

Sir Winston said in his autobiography that he married her and "lived happily ever afterwards." It was apt enough. But she never disguised the fact that life with her husband was not always easy, and once gave this advice to the girls of her old school: "If you find yourself in competition with men, never become aggressive in your rivalry. You will

141

gain more by quietly holding to your own convictions. But even this must be done with art, and above all, with conviction."

There were many occasions when I had to seek Lady Churchill's help when Sir Winston was proving difficult. She would return with me to his room and quietly tell him, "Now Winston . . ." After she had explained and reasoned with him, he invariably muttered, "Oh all right, Clemmie." He respected her advice.

XV

"We're all going to be blown up, you know"

Many people must have wondered how Sir Winston reacted to world events during the last few years of his life. The answer is that although he must have discussed them with his wife and close friends in private, he seldom commented on them. But he obviously thought about them a great deal.

I remember late one evening at the time of the Cuban crisis when Sir Winston and I were sitting together at Chartwell in front of the dying embers of the huge log fire. He had read all the newspapers during the day and fully appreciated the tenseness of the situation.

He sat in his usual armchair, very subdued. After a while he took the cigar from his mouth and said, very seriously and softly, "We are all going to be blown up, you know."

I made a light-hearted remark that, on reflection, must have seemed rather fatuous.

He appeared not to notice and heaved himself to his feet. "We're all going to be blown up," he repeated. And leaning heavily on his stick, he made his way to his bedroom. He thought, as many did at that time, that the situation would lead to war.

When President Kennedy was assassinated in Dallas, Sir Winston was in London, taking his predinner rest in his bedroom. He rarely listened to the radio and so did not hear the first news flashes. It was Lady Churchill who brought him the news. She came into his bedroom and found him reading.

"Winston," she said, "we've just heard that President Kennedy has been shot." He seemed too deeply shocked to reply. Lady Churchill told him, "We don't know the full details yet. I'll come back as soon as I hear anything."

During dinner she explained to him what she had heard on the radio, and after the meal they watched the television news together. Then she arranged for messages of sympathy to be sent to Mrs. Kennedy and the American government.

Like the rest of the world, they were both stunned by the news, and that night, after dinner, Sir Winston sat for a long time staring into the fire, pondering on the magnitude of Kennedy's death. Even so, I believe it probable that the full impact of the assassination may have been somewhat lessened because of his age.

I cannot remember seeing Sir Winston often in tears during these last years, but one was always aware of the times when he was deeply distressed. His eyes reflected the deep sadness he felt, and never so much as at the time of the death of his eldest daughter, Mrs. Diana Sandys. He was alone at his London home, Lady Churchill being in the hospital for a rest. Mr. Montague Browne brought the news to him at breakfast time.

That afternoon Sir Winston made a special point of visiting his wife. Everyone in the house felt deeply for them both and knew what a tremendous shock the death had been. She was always so alive and appeared much younger than her years.

Sir Winston was very fond of his family and nothing

pleased him more than to have them around him at Christmas or on his birthdays. He did not appear to love one more than the other, although at times I felt he had a special place in his heart for Sarah, Lady Audley.

She is a redhead like her father and with a tremendous personality; a great favorite with everyone in the household. Whenever she walked in, it was like a breath of fresh air. She has had a sad life in many ways, but she has her father's strength and certainly a great deal of her mother's charm.

Even if she did not carry the Churchill name, she would still have made an impact as an actress. Whenever she was in a play her father made great efforts to see her, even when, as in the last years, he was unable to sit through the whole show.

He always made a point of going backstage after the performance to congratulate his daughter and the cast. And his pride in her unquestionable talent was plain to see. Like him, she painted in oils, no doubt frequently picking up tips from her father. She is a beautiful woman and her shoulder-length red hair sets off her pale skin. She has exquisite taste in clothes.

Mrs. Mary Soames, Sir Winston's youngest daughter, has dark hair and some of her father's features—in complete contrast, in fact, to Sarah, who has her mother's delicate bone structure. The main quality Mrs. Soames seems to have inherited from her mother is her wonderful disposition.

Her husband, Mr. Christopher Soames, is a heavily built man, and strangely enough, rather Churchillian in appearance. Rather an extrovert, he was one of the most frequent visitors to Hyde Park Gate and his youngest son, Rupert, was a particular favorite with "Grandpapa" and "Grandmama."

Rupert and Sir Winston seemed to have a secret understanding, and they used to go up and down in the dining-room elevator holding hands. Sometimes Rupert used to perch himself on the great man's knee, and Sir Winston would pat his little fair head affectionately.

Mrs. Soames, who proved a bulwark to her mother at the end, is very close to Lady Churchill. She led a strenuous social life, being married to a man who for many years was a Cabinet Minister. Nevertheless, she did not neglect her parents, and it must have been a great comfort to them to have the five young Soames children livening up the house.

Randolph, Sir Winston's only son, has a build very much like his father's, with the same hunched shoulders. He is taller, of course. He is famous in his own right as an author and journalist and had a distinguished war record. Always a controversial figure, he often spent week-ends at Chartwell with his son, Winston.

Randolph's daughter, Arabella, visited her grandparents whenever she was on holiday from school, and Winston junior, a slim upright figure, was just as popular. Sir Winston took a keen interest in his career as a journalist, and when he wrote his first book Sir Winston was among the first to read it.

Sir Winston and Lady Churchill's children were all strik-ing personalities in their own right and lived their lives as such. But at times living in the shadow of their father must have been very difficult for them, for whatever they did or said was widely publicized. I think it is unfortunate that sometimes too much is expected of the children of great men.

Sir Winston was a wonderful subject not only for photog-raphers but also for painters and sculptors. Shortly before Christmas in 1963, a bronze head of him was sold for 2,600 guineas at Christie's. The head was by Epstein, one of an edition of ten executed in 1946. At that time this was the highest price paid for any Epstein bronze portrait. Such was the interest in the piece, sent for sale from an unnamed source, that the bidding *started* at 500 guineas. It rose rapidly, and in a matter of minutes the head was sold to Lord Bath for the record sum. He carried it away from the auction to add it to the rest of the Churchilliana he possesses. It is now the centerpiece of his collection, which he has been building up for a number of years.

Sir Winston was seldom surprised by anything, but on this occasion said one word when told of the sale: "Remarkable." He always gave the impression that he was amazed that people should pay that kind of money for a likeness of himself. "Remarkable" was one of his favorite expressions, but he was never a man to use the English language loosely and I believe he genuinely meant it.

I cannot remember ever seeing a piece of sculpture in either of Sir Winston's homes, apart from the small horse on the hall stand at Hyde Park Gate. And it always seemed strange to me that despite his love of painting, he did not collect works of art. He enjoyed viewing private collections, however, especially Somerset Maugham's at his villa in the south of France. The probable explanation for him not having his own collection is that he never had time to collect!

Any spare moments he had were spent creating works of art. His vivid impression of Chartwell in the depth of winter was widely acclaimed and hung at the Royal Academy in 1947. It was a particular favorite of his and decorated his bedroom at Hyde Park Gate. He painted Chartwell in dull red oils, the sky heavily gray with snow to come and the lawns covered in drifts. It is in some ways a depressing picture, but he obviously felt he had caught the right atmosphere.

Another of his paintings that is much admired is his view of the quayside at St. Jean, Cape Ferrat. The picture is one of many lining the corridor outside the dining room at Chartwell, and each visitor to the house always stopped to admire it, possibly because it completely captured the colorful Mediterranean setting. But the painting I most admire is a view of two trees, rocks, and a background of sea painted from the garden of Lord Beaverbrook's villa. I was with Sir Winston when he painted it.

He took four weeks to complete it, putting the finishing touches to the canvas when he returned to England. It now stands in the studio at Chartwell. He made it all look so easy. He would paint for a couple of hours, break off for lunch, and return to his canvas in the afternoon. But always it had to be when he was in the painting mood. Sometimes he spent hours looking over possible views, but this did not necessarily mean that he would return the next day to set up his easel. He used to remember the various spots and often go back months later.

He did not take up painting until he was forty, and as he once said in his book, *Painting as a Pastime,* he did not presume to explain how to paint but only how to get enjoyment. Whenever I saw him painting, I thought of that wonderful passage in his book where he described his first attempt at painting in oils: how he gingerly mixed a little blue paint on his palette with a very small brush and then, "with infinite precaution made a mark about as big as a bean on the affronted snow-white shield." He summed up the nervousness of the beginner so perfectly!

XVI

Likes and Dislikes

I THINK a comprehensive list of food that Sir Winston liked and disliked might be interesting. I can imagine some people ticking off their choices against the list.

He liked ice cream, escargots, oysters, caviar, gruyère cheese, pork cutlets, veal escalope, beef steak (medium done), any game from pheasant to woodcock, smoked and fresh salmon, *pâté de fois gras,* thick vegetable soup, trout, roast shoulder of lamb with red currant jelly, duck with orange sauce, Indian curries, squids, lobster, dressed crab, petite marmite, croutons, lightly done toast and black cherry jam, scampi, prawn cocktails, Dover soles, croissants, chocolate éclairs, cheese soufflé, meringues, creme caramel, canned pineapple, pears, asparagus tips, cauliflower with cheese sauce, spinach, broccoli, garlic, braised celery, fresh fruit salad with kirsch, pancakes, chocolate mousse, canned white peaches, runner beans, peas, oxtail, liver, steak and kidney pudding, roast beef and Yorkshire pudding, eggs in aspic, mushroom omelettes, whitebait, lump sugar, Maryland chicken, French fried and sauté potatoes, honey, venison, rum baba, apple fritters, onion soup, canned mandarin oranges, and jugged hare.

He *never* ate tripe, currant cake, marmalade, stews and hot pots, Chinese food, boiled eggs, sandwiches, lemon curd, sweet biscuits, chocolates, black puddings, apple tart, haddock and cod, muffins, crumpets, corn flakes, meat pastes, porridge, sausages, stodgy sweets, cabbage, salami, sauerkraut, pickled onions, bottled sauces, brawn, corned beef, luncheon meats, and rice pudding.

Some people might think his likes and dislikes unusual. Not many, for example, would ask for a pork chop for breakfast as he did, or fried chicken leg or lamb cutlets. He wanted something different every day, and every week I used to make out a list so that the cook could note the changes. He always ate whatever was put in front of him, but then the cook would never allow anything to go in to him that he might dislike. Just as long as the menu was not repeated two days running Sir Winston was content.

As I have said before, he never drank tea. Or cocoa. And his coffee was white for breakfast and black after lunch and dinner. It was always made from ground coffee.

He liked to drink any of the good liqueur brandies, preferably Napoleon, whisky, gin in apéritifs and cocktails, Dubonnet, the best champagnes, white wines, and occasional martinis. I never saw him drink sherry, vodka, mineral waters, beer, and the only time he drank water was a sip from a bedside glass after drinking his late night cold consomme.

He did not like noise and hated people whistling or chattering. Once, when two of his nurses were talking in his bedroom, he sighed and said, "I wish you would shut up." He objected to the noise of the *Christina*'s diesels, but obviously, short of stopping the yacht, there was little he could do about it.

He also objected to telephones ringing, and, indeed, they seldom did in either of his two homes. All calls were taken by the office switchboard between 9 A.M. and 7 P.M., afterward being switched through to the pantry where the butler took them. Consequently it was relatively quiet, so much so that one sometimes found oneself whispering when talking to another member of the staff.

Very few telephone calls were put through by the switchboard; when they were, they were usually from members of the family or close friends. Sir Winston did not have a radio until the last year of his life and even then it was not often played.

Looking back, his dislike of noise of any kind practically amounted to an obsession. He disliked the high-pitched hum of the elevator in the Hotel de Paris. His secretary finally raised the matter with the hotel manager, who was very understanding and had the elevator operating near Sir Winston's bedroom suspended every evening. Hotel guests were asked to use the other elevator.

Sir Winston was particularly allergic to high-pitched noises, which interrupted his concentration when he was trying to read in bed. He kept complaining about the whine of the elevator for some days before we were forced to take action. We were not keen to do this because we did not want to cause any inconvenience to other guests, who were paying a lot of money to stay there. However, it was obvious we should have to do something about it.

Every time Sir Winston became upset about this elevator noise, he would ring a bell to call me to his room. I used to walk in and Sir Winston, resting in bed, would say, "Stop. Listen. Can you hear anything?"

The elevator would invariably be out of use whenever he did this, so we stood for several minutes listening to nothing in particular. I really felt slightly ridiculous. I could never hear high-pitched noises anyway.

When the elevator started up Sir Winston would say, "There! Can you hear it now! Can you hear it?"

I would, of course, reply, "No, I can't, Sir Winston."

He would then look at me blankly as if I were stupid. He then said, "Ask her to come in." He never called his girl secretaries by name, always referring to the one on duty as "her," "Miss," or "the young lady."

The secretary would join us and all three of us would listen for the elevator. Minutes would go by.

As the elevator began its high-pitched whine, which was inaudible to me, Sir Winston would glare at us both and say determinedly, "THERE!"

It was almost as if he were daring us not to hear it. The girl secretary would always say, "Yes, I can hear it."

He then looked at me triumphantly and I found myself shaking my head apologetically. I never discovered if the secretary said she heard the elevator because she really did, or whether it was because of the fearsome look on Sir Winston's face.

Another thing he disliked was people tiptoeing into his room. It was as if he objected to being surprised. Anyone entering his bedroom had to do so boldly and rather noisily. It was not a question of his being deaf but simply a case of his not liking to be startled. Whenever someone did this he would give a little jump and roar at the top of his voice, "Godammit!" That one word was enough to put the fear of God into the intruder, and he would never make the same mistake again.

In the last years I always made sure that I touched him on the arm before speaking to him. For some strange reason this was acceptable. But if I suddenly spoke without warning, he would be extremely annoyed.

He intensely disliked members of his staff going off duty. Whenever this happened he would look up and say, "Can you wait a little while?" If I was going off duty or going home on holiday, even for a short weekend, he would say, "Must you?" And he would ask the other nurses afterward, "When is that boy coming back?"

He never paid compliments or gave anyone the feeling that they were indispensable. It was heart-warming to know, however, that one's absence was noticed.

Sir Winston seldom referred to me by name. If he did, it was always wrong! "Howes" was the nearest he ever got to it. I was either "that boy," "that young man," or "my man." In the last year of his life "that young man" became "that man."

He hated people fussing over him or treating him as an old man. In particular he loathed the kind of visitor who would come over to his armchair and in raised, deliberate tones say things like, "No doubt you are enjoying your well-deserved rest, Sir Winston."

This used to set him on edge. I often watched him squirm with suppressed rage, but he was too much of a gentleman to give vent to his feelings. His family never spoke to him this way, and had the over-kind visitors realized how he resented being handicapped by four strokes they would never have acted this way.

It always seems strange to me that people should immediately assume that because a person is deaf he is also slightly senile and needs to be spoken to in the simplest possible language. I only needed to pitch my voice slightly higher when speaking to Sir Winston for him to hear every word I said. I was with him day and night at different periods over the last seven years of his life, and, having had a great deal of experience with old people, I would never have described him, at any stage, as being remotely senile.

Two things let him down, his legs and his hearing. This unfortunately gave people the impression that he was just an old man obstinately clinging to life. He was acutely aware of this. And it must have been very distressing. But senility, after all, implies a state of feeble-mindedness, and he was never by any stretch of the imagination feeble-minded, even at the end.

It was sheer Churchillian guts that drove him to keep up his visits to the House of Commons, the Other Club, the Riviera. Any other man would have been broken by his setbacks. He knew precisely what was going on around him. He could have sat in an armchair and given up. He could have bought a villa in the south of France and disappeared from the public scene. But he did not.

He went on living his life to the full, right to the very end.

XVII

The Baby-Food Can

Twice a month Mr. Joe Jenner, the driver at Chartwell, used to collect a very special parcel from the local railway station. It was a blue baby-food can.

The lid was always firmly sealed and perforated and the label, stuck on with tape, read: "Sir Winston Churchill, Chartwell, Westerham, Kent." The can contained maggots. Packed in sawdust, they were in their way just as important as the seed for Toby, the parakeet.

Every time Sir Winston walked down to the fishponds, behind the rose garden, he used to throw two lidfuls to the Golden Orfe, which never failed to swim to the side whenever he approached.

The maggot can was kept on a shelf outside the policeman's lodge at the front of the house, and Sir Winston was very upset if he ever found the can empty. He never asked if there were any maggots, he assumed they would be there. When he announced, "I think I'll feed the fish," he expected me to collect half a loaf of bread from the kitchen and bring him the can.

We would set off through the front door, turning right down the side of the house and through a wrought-iron gate to the first of three fishponds. The young fish were kept in this pond and they were allowed just one lidful of maggots.

Then we continued down a rough path under an arch of rhododendrons to the second pond, which contained the fully grown Golden Orfe. Some were quite old, many were over two feet long, and one had a broken tail.

Sir Winston would sit down on a wooden seat and take the lidful of maggots to throw to the fish. After a few minutes, without saying a word, he would hold the lid out to me for me to fill up again with more maggots. It was all quite a business.

At the side of the bench was a wooden box that contained breadcrumbs, and these too were thrown to the fish. I would leave the can in the box and we would walk on down to the black swans on the small lake. The maggot can was always back on the ledge outside the policeman's lodge by the next day. Now that I come to think of it, I never really found out how it got there. But then Chartwell was so well run that even trivial details like this were taken care of.

Soon after he bought Chartwell, Sir Winston had excavated the ponds himself, together with two ornamental pools and the swimming pool. The water was pumped in a continuous circle from the two lakes, and he had even designed the layout to include a waterfall.

The next stop on our tour of the grounds was the small lake. Here Sir Winston originally had six Australian black swans and two Siberian geese, but unfortunately foxes killed the geese and three of the swans, despite all the elaborate precautions to keep them out.

One of the black swans, a huge male and rather a tyrant, always padded up to us when we drew near. Normally he was not vicious, but one day, when I had Sir Winston on one arm, the swan hit me across the wrist with his wing.

I dropped the bread and almost let go of Sir Winston as well. He was highly amused at this and thought it a great joke that "his man" should be attacked by a swan. Later it became dangerous and had to be sent away; I was not sorry to see it go. This left only two black swans, and as they showed no signs of breeding, Sir Robert Menzies, the Australian Prime Minister, arranged for a pair to be flown over from Australia. These were put on the enclosed lake, the older two being transferred to the larger one.

We would spend half an hour throwing pieces of bread to the swans, and there were so many tench and perch in the lake that they would get to the bread before the swans. Sir Winston hardly ever spoke the whole time, indeed no conversation was needed. They were delightfully lazy afternoons that we both found very relaxing.

To avoid the long climb back up to the house, a secretary used to arrange for the Hillman Husky to be left by the lake. I used to take the wheel, and with Sir Winston at my side, would drive across the meadow into the yard of Chartwell Farm, which lies behind the orchard. The farm used to belong to Sir Winston, but he sold it and it is now farmed by Eileen Joyce, the pianist, and her husband. The drive back was through the farmyard along a small lane to the main road where we always stopped because of a blind corner. Sir Winston would say, "I'll look left," but being rather apprehensive because of my passenger, I always checked myself. Whenever this happened, he would catch me looking and snap: "I said that *I* would look this way!"

There was usually a small crowd of sightseers standing at the main gates of Chartwell on summer days, taking photographs of the house. Whenever they saw Sir Winston's Cinque Ports' flag flying from the rooftop, they knew he was at home and hung about hoping to catch a glimpse of him. Few of them realized that the man they were waiting to see was approaching in the modest Hillman Husky, and it was not until we had driven through the gates and they saw him get out at the front door that they realized they had missed their chance. Perhaps they expected him to arrive in a Rolls-Royce. They were never disappointed however; Sir Winston always turned to wave to them before he went into the house.

Some weekends I would drive the great man in the Hillman Husky to the meadows on the other side of the lakes. There he would inspect his herd of Belted Galloways. I would bring the car round to the front door, collect bread from the kitchen, in case we stopped to feed the swans, and set off for the meadows with Sir Winston in the front passenger seat.

After driving slowly round the cattle we sometimes stopped to look at a newly born calf. If it was shaky on its legs Sir Winston would say, "Poor little thing."

He always acted as navigator on these afternoon trips, often pointing to rough ground, saying, "We'll go over there." We would be jolted about as the Husky bounced over the meadow, and on one occasion we nearly had an accident.

I found to my horror that I had driven down a slope to the edge of a deep hollow. The front wheels had gone partly over and I could feel scraping under the wheels. I braked immediately, intending to reverse, but he roared: "Go on, man! Forward!"

It would have been extremely dangerous had I done so. Instead, I took a deep breath and slammed the car into reverse. Fortunately we made it back up the slope.

Sir Winston simply glared at me and said impatiently, "Well, go over *there,* man," pointing in another direction.

On one of the visits to the cattle, the mother of a young calf became nervous and started to run toward our parked car. The rest of the herd followed her. I had to drive quite fast to escape them and apparently this was all seen by the secretaries at the house. They saw the Husky rocking across the meadow and became rather alarmed. Sir Winston was very amused by the incident but said nothing.

In the last year of his life when he was unable to walk great distances, Sir Winston had to use a wheelchair if he wanted to go down to the fishponds and lakes. I remember the first time he did this. Lord Montgomery was with us. I pushed Sir Winston in his chair out of the front door, but when we reached the wrought-iron gate at the side of the house we found the chair would not go through.

I suggested that Sir Winston might like to get out of the wheelchair while I folded it down. He refused to move. "It will go through," he said. I tried again and still the chair became jammed. Lord Montgomery by this time had gone on ahead to look at the fish and I began to lose my temper.

I had to tip the chair sideways, maneuvering one wheel at a time. Sir Winston continued to puff at his cigar with a slightly bored look, despite the fact that he was at an angle of nearly forty-five degrees. Eventually, after a great heave, I managed to get him through. He just looked at me calmly and said, "There you are, you see!"

Although he had the invalid chair during the last year of his life, he used a basket chair on two wheels for the last seven years whenever he felt like relaxing on the lawns. This chair enabled him to stretch out his legs, and he spent many afternoons in it, being towed around by the staff, coolie fashion.

In the spring and the late summer the detective and I would pull him across the lawns, making sure that his whisky and soda went along as well on a special garden table. Often he would only have one weak drink during the whole afternoon, but he always insisted that the whisky should be at his side. The three of us spent many hours chasing the last shafts of late afternoon sunshine so that he could enjoy the warmth as long as possible.

That is how I shall always remember him, a great hunched figure in a wicker chair; the smell of his cigar mingling with that of freshly cut grass. We had a lot of trouble lighting those cigars in strong winds, because the long Canadian matches kept blowing out. Someone gave him a box of special matches that were supposed to stay alight no matter how strong the wind, but they were not very effective. If the wind did not blow them out, Sir Winston would. He used to hold the match against the end of the cigar until the ash started to glow. Then he would take a great puff that blew the match out, scattering ash all over his coat at the same time. I finally resorted to using my gas lighter for the job.

Some days he kept both hands in his fur muff and, on other occasions, read a book, usually a period novel such as Fielding's *Tom Jones* or Scott's *Rob Roy,* while I sat behind him on the low wall regaling myself with lesser literary fare.

All I could see of him was the top of his gray Stetson, and there would be long periods of silence occasionally broken by a voice saying, "Give me a light." He never dropped off to sleep or even dozed as he sat regarding the lakes and the woods beyond. The detective, sitting a few yards away, used to listen to cricket commentaries on his transistor radio. At about half past four I would say, "May I go up to the house and have a cup of tea, Sir Winston?" And a gruff voice from under the Stetson would reply, "Ten minutes."

Lady Churchill always sat with him for half an hour or so, but being an active woman she was soon off for a walk round the garden, or else roped in the detective for a game of croquet played a hundred yards away on the other side of a private hedge.

If guests were staying at Chartwell they took turns sitting with Sir Winston, and one of the regulars was Lord Montgomery.

He had a very precise, clipped way of speaking and even behaving; very much the English gentleman, usually wearing a tweed sports coat and flannels for his weekend visits. He was thin and wiry and one felt that he had a great affection for Sir Winston, largely based on their friendship during the war years when Lord Montgomery made his name in the Western Desert by trouncing Rommel's Afrika Corps.

Lord Montgomery always sat next to his host at the dining table, and after the meal Sir Winston would sometimes turn to him, point to the brandy and say, "Will you have some of this?"

I think he did it on purpose, knowing full well that Lord Montgomery did not drink or smoke. Lord Montgomery would say: "I don't touch it," and go on to point out the wisdom of abstention. I always felt he rather liked telling people he did not drink or smoke.

He enjoyed his afternoons at Chartwell and took some very good photographs of Sir Winston and the Soames children. He excelled at photography, his main hobby.

He sometimes brought a large brown envelope with him, taking it out on the lawns whenever Sir Winston and he sat together. The envelope contained photographs of the two of them during the war years, and these pictures would set off an afternoon of reminiscences.

Lord Montgomery, his chin held high, shoulders squared and his hands clasped behind his back, used to sway slightly from heel to toe as he talked about the stories behind the pictures. Sir Winston never had any difficulty hearing his hard, penetrating voice.

They made quite a picture, the two of them on the lawns together: Montgomery, the soldier, Churchill, the statesman. Sir Winston would be sprawled at his ease in the "coolie" chair, a rug across his knees, his broad-brimmed Stetson pulled down over his eyes to shade them from the sun. Lord Montgomery used to take off his jacket on warm days and hang it on the back of his garden chair. He frequently had his camera with him and took pictures of his old friend while they reminisced. The usual items were always on the table at Sir Winston's side: the pagoda-shaped ashtray, the box of cigars, the Canadian matches, the weak whisky and soda. He rarely sat in the garden without them.

Sir Winston, it is interesting to recall, joined the army thirteen years before Lord Montgomery. One tended to forget that kind of thing watching him sit out on the lawns. It still seems incredible to me that here was a man who had not only lived through the two great world wars, but had also seen action in the Cuban Revolt of 1895, on the Indian frontier two years later, and with Kitchener in the Sudan and in the Boer War!

The old friends spent many hours by the long low wall alongside the lawn, their favorite spot. Both enjoyed talking about battles lost and won until it was time for Lord Montgomery to go indoors for tea with Lady Churchill. Sir Winston would remain on the lawn. He would go in for tea only when his grandchildren were visiting, but even then he would stick resolutely to whisky and soda.

Sir Winston loved racing and racehorses, and it was during the autumn of 1964 that he paid his last visit to his stud farm at Lingfield, Surrey. It was virtually his goodbye to his horses, because he never saw them again after that. The farm manager came to lunch one day at Chartwell and suggested that Sir Winston might like to go down, as he had not been for some time.

On the appointed day the detective drove us down in the

Humber. As we arrived, every stable boy on the stud farm was standing by his stable door ready for the inspection. Sir Winston got out of the car and seated himself on a wooden chair that had been put out in the middle of the stud yard.

A table was set up alongside it and a large plate of sliced apples put down at his elbow. The horses were paraded round the yard one at a time and then brought up to his chair for him to stroke. He gave each one a piece of apple while his manager explained about the horse's pedigree and racing potential. "I am looking forward to seeing them run," Sir Winston told him.

He wore his usual comfortable green zipper suit under a gray mottled overcoat for the visit, and his gray Stetson was pulled down over his eyes. The newspapers never got to hear about this little outing, so it was not reported. There were many such trips from Chartwell that went unnoticed.

Sometimes he went to Lord Beaverbook's country home or to Mrs. Soame's home, Hamsell Manor, at Eridge Green in Kent. He loved her children and nothing gave him greater pleasure than to sit on the lawn with them playing games. The children's nanny was always close at hand in case the children became too boisterous.

Whenever he returned to Chartwell from these outings, his black poodle Rufus was waiting for him in the hall. Sir Winston always remembered to pat him on the head when he jumped up, and on days when he went up to his study to read, Rufus trotted along with him. On the window sill in the study there was an old cigar box that was kept full of yellow dog biscuits. Sir Winston sometimes would throw one to Rufus as a special treat, but normally he did not feed him between meals.

Rufus ate his meals in the dining room with the family. He had a special cloth laid out on the Persian carpet at the side of Sir Winston's chair, and the first course was never served until the butler had given Rufus his meal. This consisted of meat scraps in a dog bowl. The butler, immaculately dressed, would ceremoniously set down the bowl and then withdraw. He was a very correct butler of the old school, rather like a "stage" butler, but unfortunately ill health forced him to give up his post. When I last heard of him he was working as Father Christmas in a Lewisham store.

Rufus had another bowl that was always kept full of water in Sir Winston's bathroom. The dog had two main meals a day at his master's side, being treated with great respect by everyone in the household. As I have said, he was eventually looked after by Miss Hamblin and because of this, stopped eating in the dining room.

A year later, after Rufus' death and the introduction of Jock, the ginger kitten, into the house, the ritual of the meal at the master's side was started again.

This time, because Jock was very young and had to be trained to stay with Sir Winston, the nurses took over the feeding and the ordering of the cat's food. Every day, when we were in London, Jock would be found sitting outside the great man's bedroom door at one o'clock, the time he knew his master would emerge and start to make his way down the corridor toward the drawing room for a pre-lunch aperitif. Jock would then walk two paces ahead, tail always carried very erect as if he were proud to be leading the way.

While Sir Winston was sitting in his armchair and sipping his drink, Jock would lie on the carpet calmly waiting for him to finish. There he stayed until the drink was finished and his master walked the twelve paces to the elevator and settled down in his chair. Jock waited until he heard the hissing noise of the elevator descending before leisurely strolling out of the drawing room across the corridor and down the stairs to the dining room.

He used to sit on the bottom step while the family took their places around the table. When all were settled, he would demand his food. I used to fetch this from the kitchens, setting the bowl down on a yellow plastic cloth decorated with a black cat. Jock then ate with the family.

In London, Jock always had other cats to play with in the next garden, but at Chartwell he used to wander off across the lawns, frequently not returning for lunch. Whenever this happened Sir Winston would look round and ask where he had gone. It meant that I or one of the other nurses had to go off looking for him. Lunch then started without the cat. Invariably we had to report that he could not be found. Afterward Sir Winston would ask, "What happened to the yellow cat?"

He never called the cat by its proper name, always using a different one: "Ginnie," "Ginger," "Pussycat," even "Yellow Dog." This last name might sound rather strange, but it was part of an elaborate game played within the family, everyone using nonsense words and expressions. Instead of saying "Hello!" for example, they said "Wow!" It was a means of identification, each person having his own nonsense word.

A member of the family, walking into the drawing room to join the others before lunch, would say "Miaow!" Then the conversation would carry on in the normal way. Although I found all this rather strange at first, I became used to it, and, in the end, found it all rather homely. After all it was not so different from the silly sayings most families are in the habit of using. They were, more than anything, words of endearment.

I remember Sir Winston saying to one of his small grandchildren, "Hello, wollygogs." The child then replied in the same cryptic vein, "Wow! Grandpapa!" He then tenderly kissed his grandfather on the cheek.

Whenever Sir Winston saw his cat stalk through the bedroom door he said, "Miaow! Pussycat!"

Jock would sometimes jump up onto the bed and try to take a nap between the great man's feet. He was never able to stay there long, however. Sir Winston would wiggle his toes to move Jock over. With half an eye open, the cat used to bite through the sheets and sink his teeth into his master's feet. Later I would find red marks on Sir Winston's ankles. "You really must stop playing with Jock like this," I told him. He never took any notice. "Nonsense," he said.

Jock never slept on the bed at night for this reason. He used to lie on an armchair next to the night nurse, who was posted in the study. He was good company because there were times when bats got in and started flying about in the rafters. Jock would jump onto the table to try and reach them, and we then hurriedly had to remove the framed pictures and other knicknacks on the table. Some of the female nurses were rather nervous, and I can understand why. With a small night lamp, the study took on an eerie appearance in the early hours, and the intruders made flapping noises as they flew against the flags decorating the ceiling.

All the time Sir Winston would be asleep in his bedroom just through the curtained archway from the study. He seldom woke up in the night and the nurse on duty had long stretches with little to do except read a book, make cups of coffee in the kitchen down the corridor, and watch out for bats.

XVIII

"It comes to all of us"

ONE day in February 1964, the last year of Sir Winston's life, Mr. Harold Macmillan called for lunch at Hyde Park Gate. It was his first visit since his resignation as Prime Minister.

"Sorry to hear you're out of office now," said Sir Winston.

Mr. Macmillan shrugged his shoulders and replied, "Well, it comes to all of us, doesn't it?" And they sat down to roast beef and Yorkshire pudding.

It was a touching moment. Side by side, tucking into their meal, were two former leaders of the nation who now had to watch the world from the sidelines.

Mr. Macmillan, like Sir Winston, had been a wonderful subject for the political cartoonists while he was Prime Minister. In real life he seemed almost a caricature of himself with his droopy moustache, elegant sweeps of gray hair above his ears and deep, resonant voice.

After lunch they drove down to the House of Commons together for Question Time. Their entrance into the Chamber, Sir Winston leaning on his old friend's arm, was quite nostalgic. One observer recorded that it was "as if someone had thrown a switch to illuminate the proceedings."

Throughout the first half of the year Sir Winston was in his seat at least once a week, taking a keen interest in the proceedings. On one visit he told the M.P. sitting next to him, "You know, there aren't the speakers in the House today that there used to be." Another time, after a young member had asked a question, Sir Winston enquired about the name of the newcomer. When told, he replied, "It was a damn fool question."

He knew he would soon be giving up his seat and certainly intended making the most of his last term as an M.P. One week he was in the Chamber on three successive days. Everyone could see the difficulty he had in getting about, but although he was brought to the door in a wheelchair he insisted, with typical determination, on walking across the floor to his place on the Front Bench below the gangway.

He frequently surprised and delighted members on both sides by voting in more than one division and was obviously determined to set an example to some of the younger Tory back-benchers. It was, of course, not really expected of him to respond to the division bells on routine matters, but his attitude was one of, "While I can walk, I will."

He seemed to take on the role of a benevolent grandfather whenever he was in the Commons, and as he sat on the Front Bench it seemed almost as if the House was his family.

He made his last appearance on July 27th, 1964. When he left his front-row corner seat, he was helped along by two fellow M.P.s, turning to make the usual bow of recognition to the Speaker. The tributes poured in from every side, but I think the last one, from Mr. Macmillan, was probably the finest. He said: "The life of the man whom we are today honoring is unique. The oldest among us can recall nothing to compare with it and the younger ones among you, however long you live, will never see the like again."

Politicians abroad were equally aware of the debt they owed him. Indeed, Fidel Castro once told a group of young Cubans, "If Churchill had not done what he did to defeat the Nazis, you wouldn't be here—none of us would. We have to take a special interest in him because he, too, led a little island against a great enemy."

Sir Winston read the reports of this speech when he went through the morning papers after breakfast, and I know he was very pleased. He made no comment, but his reaction was plain. He had a great admiration for the leaders of nations, regardless of their politics.

He no longer spoke in the Commons, of course, and it is something to be thankful for that his great speeches have been recorded. Sir Winston was presented with an album of his speeches, and he played them over on many afternoons while sitting in the drawing room of his London home. He also played them there in the evening, after dinner, always on his portable record player, which was kept in the bedroom.

I used to bring the record player along and set it up on a small table in front of him as he sat before the fire. He did not have a cabinet for his records, which were stacked on the floor under the writing desk in his room. Whenever he felt like a session I picked out the records, usually selecting half a dozen.

He had a complete set of music from the Gilbert and Sullivan operas but they were on the old-fashioned twelve-inch records, some of which were well worn. They were gradually being replaced by long-playing versions given him as birthday and Christmas presents.

Also in his collection of records were marches by the Brigade of Guards' Massed Bands; the original Broadway stage version of Rodgers and Hammerstein's *The King and I*, with Gertrude Lawrence; Noel Coward recorded at the Café de Paris; and the Harrow School songs. As he sat listening to these he used to tap his foot in time with the music.

Whenever he listened to his speeches he was completely absorbed: his cigar would go out, he forgot his favorite pastime of raking the fire with his walking stick, and the whisky was ignored. If the butler brought in the evening newspapers, instead of reading them immediately as he usually did, Sir Winston put them on the table at his side without a word until his speeches had finished.

I always made a point of playing the speeches through in strict rotation as I wanted to hear them as much as he did. One afternoon when we were both sitting together listening to them, Miss Hamblin, who had been Sir Winston's secretary during the war, put her head round the door. She told me the story behind the speech we were hearing.

She said she had worked on it with him until half past one in the morning and still he was not satisfied with the finished article. "Come back at half past eight," he told her, and she went home leaving him with her typewritten notes.

When she returned, Sir Winston was sitting up in bed reading the papers. "I have finished it," he said triumphantly. "I wrote it myself." She found that he had completely rewritten the speech.

He had done it in longhand and it must have taken him considerable time, leaving only two or three hours for sleep. The speech had to be finished because he was due to give it at the Mansion House that day. Miss Hamblin was naturally very proud that she had been able to help with it.

By April 1964 Sir Winston's public appearances were less frequent. He still went to the House of Commons some afternoons and managed regularly to attend dinners of the Other Club, but outings other than these were rare.

However, he did make a special effort to see his daughter, Sarah, in *Fata Morgana,* the Hungarian comedy, when it was put on at the modern Ashcroft Theatre in Croydon. It was the last time he saw her on the stage and indeed his last visit to a theatre.

It was felt that a play running for two and a half hours would be too much for him to sit through, so arrangements were made for him to join his wife in the stalls after the first act. Sarah was making her first stage appearance after the death of her husband, Lord Audley, the previous July, and when the curtain came down, her parents were backstage as usual to congratulate her and the cast.

The management thought they had done the right thing when they offered their distinguished guest a very large whisky and soda in a stemmed glass. This may have been in line with the public image, but in fact he left most of it. Strange as it may seem, he never drank large whiskies and sodas; a three-ounce glass would last him for two to three hours. He was a firm believer in never hurrying his drinks. If he were drinking a whisky and going out for the evening, he often left it rather than finish it quickly. This was important to him. I remember the times he poured me a drink and how he always watched carefully to see that it was savored properly. Similarly, when he offered me cigars, they had to be pierced and lit the Churchill way.

Sir Winston, as I have said, was unable to attend the inauguration of Churchill College, Cambridge, but it was an even bigger disappointment when he was unable to attend the official opening in 1964. The journey would have been too much. Four members of the family represented him: Lady Churchill, Mrs. Soames, Randolph Churchill and his son Winston.

The opening ceremony was performed by the Duke of Edinburgh, who, in his speech, referred to Sir Winston's inspiration during the war and very aptly summed up one of his characteristics. "He had an unerring instinct for the heart of the matter," the Duke said. "He had that essential ability in his thinking which cut through all the dead wood of accepted practice and the blind unreasoning 'fellowship' which inhibits any kind of progress.

"He could peel away the layers of habitual thought like a chef peeling an onion. This is real discrimination, which is so much more valuable than the automatic acceptance of anything new and the facile rejection of anything old."

The Duke said the college was intended to be "the national tribute and ultimate memorial to one of the really great men in our history."

Apart from being absent at the opening of the college that year, Sir Winston also missed the wedding of his twenty-three-year-old grandson, Winston. He married Miss Minnie d'Erlanger, who was a year older and the daughter of the late Sir Gerard d'Erlanger, former chairman of B.O.A.C. The ceremony at Kensington register office was a quiet affair and only lasted ten minutes.

Before the big hotel reception, Winston junior took his bride to Hyde Park Gate for champagne and toasts with his grandfather. Sir Winston smiled benevolently and kissed the bride before they moved out into the tiny garden to pose for photographs. Everyone remarked on the close resemblance between young Winston and his grandfather in his early army days: Winston had the same jutting jaw and upright carriage.

Chairs were carried out of the house for the family photograph, which was taken by Karsh. In the center of the group was Sir Winston, who had Jock on his lap. He was flanked by the bride and bridegroom. Mrs. Leland Hayward, Randolph Churchill's ex-wife and mother of

Winston junior, stood immediately behind her son, at the side of Lady Churchill.

It was a day the great man was determined not to miss. Because he could not venture far, the reception, as it were, came to him. He found his new granddaughter-in-law enchanting and made it quite obvious that he was all in favor of the match. She looked very beautiful indeed.

A few days after the wedding Sir Winston had important visitors at Hyde Park Gate. They arrived in two large cars and brought with them a green leather-covered folder, lined in silk and bearing the Commons crest. Printed in gold on the cover were the words, "Vote of thanks to the Right Hon. Sir Winston Churchill, K.G., O.M., C.H., M.P."

The visitors were Sir Alec Douglas-Home, then Prime Minister, Mr. Harold Wilson, Mr. Jo Grimond, Sir Thomas More, and Mr. Emanuel Shinwell. They constituted a specially appointed committee to hand over the Commons tribute to Sir Winston on his retirement from Parliament. The tribute, printed on velum, is worth recording, for it sums up so well the feelings of everyone.

It read: "That this House desires to take this opportunity of marking the forthcoming retirement of the Rt. Hon. Gentleman, the Member for Woodford, by putting on record its unbounded admiration and gratitude for his services to Parliament, to the nation and to the world; remembers above all his inspiration of the British people when they stood alone, and his leadership until victory was won; and offers its grateful thanks to the Rt. Hon. Gentleman for these outstanding services to the House and to the nation."

This was, I believe, the method chosen by the House in the nineteenth century when a tribute was presented to the Duke of Wellingon. As the visitors toasted Sir Winston in champagne, he was very touched and near to tears. It was one more sad moment in his life.

That last summer there seemed to be constant reminders that, at the end of the year, Sir Winston would be ninety. The newspapers always seemed to be carrying small paragraphs, usually well toward the bottom of the page, about the deaths of men who, in all kinds of different ways, had been connected with him.

He was, as I have said, the sole surviving officer of the cavalry charge at Omdurman. It seemed hard to believe that he had lived through so many wars and that his life span stretched from "fuzzy-wuzzies" with spears, to spacemen and hydrogen bombs. One of the news items that summer recorded the death, at ninety, of Jan Van Bloemenstein, a Boer War veteran who escorted the young Churchill to Pretoria after his capture in Natal. Yet another link with the past had been swept away.

I remember thinking as we sat on the lawns at Chartwell that the whole of this man's life was building up to a tremendous climax. What a life it had been! And what a finale! A poll taken in America showed that, after President Johnson, the man the Americans most admired was Sir Winston. I believe that, had a world poll been carried out, he would have led the field.

XIX

"Oh! You're getting saucier!"

THE nursing staff around Sir Winston in the last years had a very difficult task. The family felt that if we were too conspicuous it would appear that he was in very poor mental and physical health, and consequently we stayed in the background, often mistaken for housemaids or secretaries. I know that at various times many people thought I was a detective helping Sergeant Murray, a valet hovering around his master, or even the chauffeur.

Other members of the household saw only the legend; we had to deal with the man. Our main job was not to cure his ills but to see that he did not *become* ill. And to do this we had to keep a twenty-four-hour watch; we also had to take a strictly clinical line. We could not possibly look upon him with the reverence held by long-serving members of the staff.

Although he had given me numerous autographed copies of his books, I purposely did not begin to read them until after his death. How could I possibly have done my job had I allowed the legend to take over from the man? It would have been so easy to have made this mistake.

As I have said, Sir Winston's personality sapped the

energies of all those around him. It was like a game of chess. If he agreed to do something with little persuasion, one always knew that he had an ulterior motive. He would say, "All right, I'll have the pills," and invariably, shortly afterward, would announce that he intended taking a bath when he knew that this was expressly forbidden by his doctors. On other occasions when he gave in readily to our suggestions, it was simply an indication that he intended breaking the rules later by wanting to get up for a meal.

We sometimes had to make a deal with him when he was ill. I knew he dearly loved his bath and occasionally allowed him to have one, against the doctors' orders, on condition that he continued a more important part of the treatment. Once he gave his word he would do a thing, he stood by it.

It was pointless telling him that he had to follow the doctors' instructions. Even if I called in the doctor and Sir Winston agreed to do what he said, I knew that as soon as he left the bedroom we were back where we started. There were times when we had to resort to asking Mr. Montague Browne to speak to him, but that was not always a success. Our last resort was to call in Lady Churchill.

I do not want to give the impression that he was merely a difficult old man. He enjoyed these clashes and had a great deal of respect for us when we held our ground. Nevertheless he was an expert in coming out on top! Let me explain.

I would say, "Here's your tablet."

"What's it for?"

I would explain at length that it would relieve a certain ailment.

"How?"

I would launch into another lengthy explanation at the end of which Sir Winston would look at me blandly and say, "In which way?"

I used to sink deeper and deeper into a tangle of explanations until, in sheer desperation, I said, "Well, you've only got to take them for another two days."

He took them in the end, but it was always with a glint in his eyes which made it clear that, as far as he was concerned, he had won the round.

I never wore a white coat or any form of uniform, and although the female nurses wore uniforms in various pastel shades, they did not have the traditional cap and apron. One nurse, who was with us a short time, continued to wear a severe blue dress with a starched collar, but she was an exception. Most of us tried to be as inconspicuous as possible.

Of course Sir Winston was not always aggressive and domineering. There were days when he was very humorous. On one of these occasions I was working with a new girl who had a lively and vivacious personality, which, I am pleased to say, she did not suppress.

Shortly after she started, Sir Winston was sitting in the armchair in his bedroom, and we told him the family was waiting in the drawing room. The new nurse was standing in his way as he got up, so he jokingly prodded her with his walking stick. She gasped, "Oh! You're getting saucier!"

No one ever spoke to him that way, and I thought she had overstepped the mark. I waited for the great man to fire a broadside. But instead of the expected roar of rage he simply leaned forward and said to her, "And you're . . . getting *uglier!*"

All three of us burst into laughter and the incident passed off quite pleasantly. But this kind of thing brought frowns of disapproval from others in the house. For them, familiarity was definitely out; perhaps that is why we were not very popular, for we were too close.

In the last years he did not have a valet, and all his personal needs, including the pressing of his clothes, were undertaken by the nursing staff. As the senior, most of the work fell on my shoulders, but the others helped and never considered it below them. On two of the cruises, because of tight accommodation on the yacht, Fritz Schmied, the chef, helped me as a "night nurse." We occupied a double cabin next to Sir Winston's and after the trips Schmied, who was excellent as a chef, went back to the kitchens.

While I was quite prepared to act as Sir Winston's valet, I found that at one stage I was working practically round the clock, so a valet was engaged. He stayed only four days, making it quite clear that he was not prepared to be on call twenty-four hours a day. He told me that he found the household quite extraordinary. He had never worked for a family that commuted twice weekly between two establishments and found the constant packing nerve-racking. For example, instead of taking an overnight bag down to the country, ten pieces of luggage went down for Sir Winston alone. With Lady Churchill's luggage, and the staff's luggage, it was quite a load.

It is difficult to describe the variety of things that were constantly being shuttled backward and forward between the two houses, but the sight of them being loaded up evidently frightened the four-day valet. I imagine that seeing this amount of luggage assembled for a weekend in the country must have made him wonder what the family took with them when they traveled abroad.

When Sir Winston left for a trip abroad it was usually at a week's notice. Although the secretarial staff knew the dates, these were kept secret because for some unknown reason it was not thought advisable for the press to know in advance. Fifteen pieces of luggage were taken, and they included such minor items as his two feather pillows, two blue blankets, fuel for his handwarmer, sponges, and bath thermometers. Perhaps the routine accounted for the fact that few nurses stayed more than six months.

One who stayed over a year was a tall redhead, Miss Wendy Bunford, who came from a village in Surrey. She went on two of the later cruises, accompanied on one by Miss McAlpin, and also made numerous visits to the Riviera. With her quiet, efficient manner, she was more successful than anyone in persuading Sir Winston to follow the doctors' orders. Nothing ruffled her, and she took him completely in her stride. It was almost as if she refused to be awed. She always smiled politely when he made a pun, which was one of his favorite pastimes. And when he was in a difficult mood and proving impossible, she refused to rise to the bait, carrying on steadily as if there were no problem.

She left to marry a Norwegian, and on the day she handed in her notice, Sir Winston was genuinely upset. He told her, "My dear, I hear you are leaving us. I am very sorry." Miss Bunford was the only nurse who, after she left, always received one of his special cards at Christmas.

The nurses never obtruded. They spent their time with Sir Winston quietly reading or writing letters. I remember one occasion when we were together in the drawing room at Hyde Park Gate shortly before his ninetieth birthday. He suddenly looked up and asked me out of the blue, "What are you doing?" I told him that I was writing to my mother, who had been ill.

"You may say that I hope she has recovered now," he told me. I thanked him and wrote that he sent his best wishes. It was a typical gesture and an example of the flashes of old-world courtesy he sometimes showed.

Sir Winston was always interested in the people around him and where they came from. One day he asked me, "Where is your home?" I said it was in Haverfordwest, Wales. The next day I was off duty and when I returned, he asked me where I had been. I told him that I had spent the day at home.

Rather dryly he said, "Rather a long way to go for one day, wasn't it?" He knew very well, of course, that I meant my London flat.

Sir Winston, who outlived his old friend Lord Beaverbrook by seven months, was very distressed when he heard that "Max," as he called him, was dead. He was in London when his secretary broke the news.

Mr. Montague Browne told him as gently as possible. He gave his usual light knock on the bedroom door and walked straight in. Sir Winston was in bed reading the newspapers.

"I'm sorry to have to tell you this, Sir Winston," he said. "We have just heard that Max is dead."

Sir Winston did not reply. He just put down his book and bowed his head as the secretary tactfully withdrew to leave him with his thoughts. For the rest of the day he scarcely spoke to anyone, and a great depression seemed to settle over the house. The fact that he was silent was in itself significant. This was his way with grief. Lord Beaverbrook, without any doubt, had been his greatest friend. They had a mutual respect for one another, and whenever they sat down for a meal at the same table one felt the bond between them. That day in June, my mind went back to the happy times at La Capponcina.

I remembered them sitting together on the little shaded terrace at the front of the villa, Sir Winston with his giant white Stetson and Lord Beaverbrook wearing a Panama hat with the brim turned down all round. And I remembered the times they used to joke about Sir Winston using the electric chair-elevator on the long stairway at the villa.

This had been installed for Lord Beaverbrook, who suffered from regular asthmatic attacks. Whenever his old friend was visiting him, however, he allowed him to use it, padding up the stairs behind him. Lord Beaverbrook used to say, "Off you go, Winston, I'll see you at the top." At every few steps, however, Sir Winston stopped the elevator for his host to catch up, both of them chuckling at the little race.

It was one of the few times I ever heard Sir Winston laugh; simple things like this amused him. He always seemed to be far more relaxed when he was with Lord Beaverbrook, who never gave the impression that he was striving to entertain him. There were never any elaborate arrangements made when they were both at the villa. The days passed by with each pleasing himself about how he spent his time.

It was very different from the nervous tension that sometimes developed when the Churchill entourage was staying elsewhere. It all stemmed from the fact that most people looked upon the great man as a piece of history, something to be handled with care.

Sir Winston's staff found Lord Beaverbrook rather harsh and demanding. We were used to obstinacy but not to this. He was tough and iron-willed and only seemed interested in complete efficiency. A friend once complained to him that one of his reporters had overstepped the mark by pushing too hard on a story. Lord Beaverbrook simply laughed, and replied, "When they *stop* pushing too hard, then I'll be worried."

Even when Lord Beaverbrook was not staying at his villa, Sir Winston made frequent visits to La Capponcina from Monte Carlo, sometimes to set up his easel and paint, on other occasions just to sit in the garden enjoying the sunshine and the view. On cold winter days in London, he used to look out of the window and say, "I must go to France." But after the death of Lord Beaverbrook in June 1964, he never talked about going abroad again.

XX

A Ninetieth Birthday

THE greatest landmark in the latter years of **Sir** Winston's life was undoubtedly his ninetieth birthday. It was a day he thoroughly enjoyed, one he spent with his family at Hyde Park Gate, in London.

The excitement really began on the day before the 30th of November 1964, when a crowd gathered outside the front door, packing the cul-de-sac for two hours to catch a glimpse of Sir Winston as he posed at the front windows for the benefit of the press photographers.

He rose at his usual time, about 12:15 P.M., had his bath, and climbed into a brand-new green velvet siren suit. He had eight of them, specially made by a City tailor in exactly the same style as his famous wartime zipper suits.

There was some discussion between Lady Churchill and myself about what he should wear for the birthday pictures. Knowing that Sir Winston liked the comfort of the siren suits, I produced the green one from his wardrobe. He always enjoyed wearing these because they were comfortable and easy to slip on.

The people in the street had read in the Saturday morning newspapers that he would be at his window at 1 P.M.

and began to gather at midday on the pavement on both sides of the road. Inside the house Lady Churchill kept popping into the bedroom to see if her husband was ready and then, before he walked out, leaning on his stick, she gave him a last check-over to make sure that he looked his best.

Although ninety, Sir Winston still reacted very strongly to crowds. He leaned on the sill as the window was opened, beaming and waving as the crowd shouted, "Happy birthday, sir!"

The crowds had been standing in driving rain and broke into a spontaneous chorus of "For he's a jolly good fellow." Sir Winston brushed aside my supporting arm with a flash of the old fire to acknowledge the applause.

He spread his arms wide as if embracing the crowd when they sang "Happy birthday, dear Winston, happy birthday to you," and there was a good deal of good-natured pushing and shoving as the people tried to get a better view. Some people at the back complained that the photographers against the house rails were in the way; one man was roundly abused because he insisted on keeping his umbrella up!

We had made sure that the curtains of the drawing room were kept drawn until Sir Winston was in position and the sudden action of pulling them back, revealing him standing there smiling, added a theatrical touch that was quite justifiable. This was what the hundreds of patient well-wishers had been waiting for. Through all the excitement he stood smiling and waving back in acknowledgement, no doubt touched to see so many young people and mothers with babies in the crowd.

The curtains drifted together and the people must have thought Sir Winston had finished waving. But a few moments later he returned to the window to lean out jauntily to rounds of further applause. He then went back into the drawing room and Lady Churchill finally called out to the crowd, "Sir Winston would like to come to the window again but he cannot. He heard you all singing and thanks you very much." She closed the window with a smile, saying gently but firmly, "Quiet now, please."

It was a remarkable display of affection, and Sir Winston had tears in his eyes as he turned from the window. The crowd's singing and enthusiasm meant a lot.

He was genuinely touched that people should still have a warm affection for him. After all, it had been some time since he last had a crowd cheering him. Although people always gathered outside the house for his birthday, this was a very special occasion. The last time there had been so many admirers was on his discharge from the Middlesex Hospital two years earlier after his fall in the south of France.

This particular morning Sir Winston had his usual Dubonnet before sitting down to a roast beef lunch. Afterward I sat with him in the drawing room while he had his coffee and cognac, watching a half-hour American TV film, "Sea Hunt," with Lloyd Bridges. He always had a rest in the afternoon from 5 P.M. until dinner at 8:15 P.M., but that day he missed his early evening nap. Instead he had dinner at 7 P.M. so that he could watch the BBC tribute "Ninety Years On," the star-packed variety show introduced by Noel Coward, linked with a commentary written by Terence Rattigan. It went on for ninety-five minutes, with Coward speaking directly to Sir Winston as he introduced the long string of top entertainers who recalled the hit tunes over the past ninety years. Sir Winston, Lady Churchill, and their daughter Sarah watched the program from the dining table as they drank their after-dinner coffee. He enjoyed the program immensely and kept tapping his foot in time with the nostalgic melodies.

Practically every top variety artist took part in the television tribute. Kathy Kirby played Marie Lloyd, the queen of the halls, and sang her famous "Me Old Cock Linnett" ... Cicely Courtneidge, dressed as a guardsman, impersonated Ella Shields for "Soldiers of the Queen" ... Billy Cotton, the band leader, sang Harry Champion's "Any Old Iron" ... Alma Cogan flew specially from Australia to play Florrie Forde, singing "Down at the Old Bull and Bush" ... Arthur Askey played Billy Merson and sang his famous comedy number "The Spaniard Who Blighted My Life" ... Jimmy Edwards, his mustache more magnificent than ever, was George Laybourne and sang "Champagne Charlie."

Ted Ray and Wilfred Brambell impersonated Will Hay and Moore Marriott in one of their famous classroom sketches ... Margot Fonteyn appeared briefly as Anna Pavlova ... Anton Rodgers played the great music hall comic, Dan Leno ... Edmund Hockeridge sang one of Sir Winston's favorite songs, "Oh What a Beautiful Morning."

Each tune must have brought memories flooding back ... Harry Secombe, dressed as a First World War Tommy, sang "Roses of Picardy" ... Noel Coward sang his famous "Mad Dogs and Englishmen" ... It was exactly the type of entertainment he liked.

He retired early at 10:30 P.M. Exactly twelve hours later I woke him on his ninetieth birthday, drew back the curtains, and said, "May I wish you many happy returns, sir." I thought back to his eighty-fourth birthday when I had nervously wished him a happy birthday and he had replied, "Many happy returns? At eighty-four I shouldn't think there will be many more."

This time he just smiled faintly and thanked me. I pressed the wall buzzer, which warned the butler that he was awake and required breakfast. Sir Winston sat up in bed wearing a blue bed jacket over a silk vest. His Spanish butler, Enrique, brought the breakfast in on a large wooden tray covered with a white napkin.

Sir Winston tucked into buttered toast with apricot jam, which was a change from the black cherry jam he usually liked. He drank a cup of coffee, then turned to the newspapers. All the front pages seemed to be carrying the pictures of him waving at the window, and some were exceptionally good. He made no comment but read every word about his birthday.

As usual, he went systematically through the pile of newspapers while I went off to look for the cat. Sir Winston never skimmed through the morning papers; he went through them with great care. He rarely bothered to look at the comic strips but always showed great interest in the political cartoonists.

Sir Winston had only got as far as *The Times* when Lady Churchill came in. She first put her head round the doorway and, seeing that he was awake, went over to his side and kissed him lightly on the forehead. "Good morning, darling," she said. "Many happy returns."

Then she sang "Happy birthday to you" in a soft, sweet voice, which brought the response, "That was lovely." Lady Churchill kissed her husband again, waved her hand as if to say, "I'll see you later," and swept out of the bedroom door, only to return almost immediately to ask me if I would help carry in the Queen's flowers.

They had already been taken out of their cellophane wrapping and put in a large white china vase. I carried them into Sir Winston's room and put them on the dressing table immediately in front of the bed while Lady Churchill showed her husband the accompanying card.

It was headed Buckingham Palace and read: "To Sir Winston, with my sincere good wishes and congratulations on your ninetieth birthday, from Elizabeth R."

These were exotic flowers with long green stems. We

were rather puzzled by them, no one knowing their name. Lady Churchill said she knew but could not remember and everyone else was rather vague. Later we discovered that they were "Birds of Paradise" flowers. The Queen also sent a large bunch of freesias, which were also put on the dressing-table.

Lady Churchill had already given her husband her birthday present the night before. It was a small gold heart framing two numbers, "90," to be attached to his watch-chain next to the other small gold heart, which was her engagement present.

All the world's statesmen sent their greetings, by cable and special envoy. There were messages from President Johnson, who asked America to celebrate the day as "Sir Winston Churchill Day," the Pope, President de Gaulle, Marshal Tito, Dr. Adenauer, and many others.

President Johnson invited Americans to mark the day with special ceremonies, describing the birthday as a significant milestone in Sir Winston's life, one certainly deserving special recognition. He recalled that Sir Winston was an honorary citizen of his country, and indeed the Americans celebrated the occasion as much as people in this country. Practically every U.S. television network carried special commemorative programs. Only one country refrained from paying tribute: Russia. The Government newspaper blamed Sir Winston for starting the cold war by coining the phrase "The Iron Curtain"!

One of the most interesting messages was from South Africa. The Mayor of Pretoria sent a cable saying that his city was proud to recall that it was the only capital to have been host to him as "an unwilling guest" in the Boer War.

All the continental newspapers published reports and photographs to mark the day, and these were shown to Sir Winston. One French newspaper mentioned his wartime speeches and described how they had heartened the French during the German occupation. They called him "the old British lion with a stormy and glorious life."

The Germans spoke of the great services he had performed for the Atlantic Alliance and European unification. The Italians said that had Sir Winston been twenty years younger he would have been the one Englishman capable of guiding Britain toward taking part in a united Europe.

The Commonwealth countries were equally enthusiastic. The Governor-General of Canada cabled: "Canada and the free world owe you a debt of gratitude for your leadership, integrity and courage." The Prime Minister of New Zealand spoke of his country's deep affection and respect for "your personal qualities and the great part you have played in the history of our time." Sir Winston's great friend, ex-President Eisenhower, paid this personal tribute: "He came to typify for me Britain's courage and perseverance in adversity, its conservatism in success, its valid pride in the glories of the past, its vision of future leadership responsibilities in the family of nations. . . . He was an authentic spokesman for Britain's greatness of spirit. I cherish the warm friendship I enjoy with him. Americans prize his ancestral association with them. With all my heart I wish him a happy birthday."

There were over 70,000 birthday cards, messages and telegrams. So many, in fact, that it was physically impossible for Sir Winston to read all of them. The presents were piled high in the corridor outside the main office, and the secretaries were continually kept busy opening them and setting out the ones to be shown to Sir Winston.

Randolph gave his father two solid gold ashtrays engraved with the family crest. Winston, his son, and his wife Minnie, gave an antique solid silver handbell, also engraved with the crest. Baroness Asquith gave the present she always gave Sir Winston on his birthday: a posy of violets. Sir Anthony Eden presented Sir Winston with a first edition of Lord Byron's *Childe Harold's Pilgrimage*. On the fly-leaf he wrote, "Winston, with affectionate greetings from Anthony and Clarrisa."

While some of the presents were extremely valuable, others were, to put it mildly, rather unusual. One American tobacco firm sent Sir Winston packets of Turkish filter-tip cigarettes. This was rather odd as I had never seen Sir Winston smoke a cigarette all the time I worked for him, and I do not believe he ever did in the latter years. Someone else sent him a leather bulldog, two feet high; it was rather difficult to recognize as a bulldog. Another present was an enormous candle and stand decorated with religious pictures. The most unusual present was from admirers in Ireland. They sent Sir Winston half a dozen potatoes, one swede, and a few carrots and tomatoes, all neatly packed in layers of peat.

The Jamaican High Commissioner sent a beautifully ornate box with a lock and key containing fifty Jamaican cigars. Boxes of cigars poured in, all to be stacked away in the cupboard until Sir Winston needed them. There was a special box of fifty cigars with a silver plate screwed on the lid; the inscription read: "Sir Winston Churchill, from the Swedish Cigar Club."

Among the many presents was a set of three gold medallions, especially struck to commemorate the ninetieth birthday. It was from a City of London firm of bankers. The coins bore a profile of Sir Winston on one side with the quotation, "This was their finest hour," on the reverse. Copies of these, minted in Austria, were immediately sold and will probably be worth large sums to collectors. Rarely is such a compliment paid during the lifetime of a great man.

Sarah gave her father one of her paintings, a landscape with a bird perched in a tree in the foreground. Like Sir Winston, she was an exceptionally fine painter, all her work being characterized by particularly delicate brush-work. Mr. Jock Colville gave a year's subscription to *The Illustrated London News*. One of the most unusual presents, and one that made a big impression on Sir Winston, was a gold cage with a mechanical whistling bird inside. It was from Mrs. d'Erlanger, mother of Winston junior's bride.

The Soames gave cigars and bath cologne, as did many others. Altogether Sir Winston had over five hundred presents, more than twice the number he normally received on his birthday.

Sir Winston shaved, bathed and then went back to bed. It had previously been decided that he should have lunch in bed on his birthday in order to conserve his energies for a large family dinner party in the evening.

Headed by Lady Churchill and Mr. Montague Browne, ten members of the staff then trooped into the bedroom. Everyone individually wished him a happy birthday before Enrique brought in a magnum of Kruger champagne. Sir Winston sat up in bed, beamed at the assembled company, and held out his glass. The bedroom visitors sang "Happy birthday to you," then drank a toast proposed by Lady Churchill.

She thanked everyone for looking after Sir Winston so well for so long. "I know you do it because you love him so," she said. Lady Churchill and Mr. Montague Browne sat at a small round table at the side of the bed, joining Sir Winston for a lunch of lamb cutlets, peas, and potatoes. Another bottle of champagne was opened.

Lady Churchill went to her room to rest, and the secretary returned to work while Sir Winston prepared for his next visitor: Mr. Harold Wilson, Prime Minister of the new Labor government.

Promptly at 3 P.M. the crowd outside, most of whom had been there for four hours, began cheering and photographers' flashbulbs went off as Mr. Wilson stepped from his car.

He went straight into Sir Winston's bedroom, walked over to the bedside and shook his hand, wishing him a happy birthday. Sir Winston was resplendent in a red paisley smoking jacket of which he was very proud. Lady Churchill had given it to him for his previous birthday, and he always made a point of wearing it to receive special guests.

Mr. Wilson said, "I bring you the good wishes of the Cabinet." Sir Winston thanked him. Lady Churchill, who had taken the Prime Minister into the bedroom, began reminiscing about Chequers and asked Mr. Wilson how the garden was looking, before they toasted Sir Winston in brandy.

Sir Winston replied with a toast to the new government. The Prime Minister then left and Sir Winston turned his attention to the thousands of letters and telegrams that had been steadily arriving. Six girl secretaries worked solidly throughout the day in the Hyde Park Gate office sifting the mass of mail, drafting replies, and picking out important messages to be taken into the bedroom.

The bed and the bedtable that ran across it were swamped with telegrams and letters. Sir Winston, a whisky and soda in hand, and his cigar firmly clamped between his teeth, read them as they were brought to him.

His birthday cake, made as always by Madame Floris, arrived and was put in the dining room. The idea was to spread the surprises; he was not to see the cake until he went in for dinner. It was an enormous cake, weighing 120 pounds and covered in white royal icing. There was a golden rose at its center, surrounded by acorns and oak leaves in marzipan, and it contained thirty pounds of fruit and fifty eggs.

On a scroll in front of the cake were his famous words,

"In war—resolution, in defeat—defiance, in victory—magnanimity, in peace—goodwill."

They were taken from the first volume of Sir Winston's *The Second World War*.

Around the cake, the twenty-third made by the firm for Sir Winston, were the words "Happy birthday," in white lettering, offset by a broad ribbon in gold satin.

It really was a magnificent effort on the part of the royal cakemakers, and the theme of oak and acorn was most appropriate.

The front door was continually swinging open and shut as slightly nervous maids shuttled back and forth carrying large bouquets, telegrams, letters, parcels. One postcard stood out. It was addressed to "The Greatest Man Alive, W.S.C. London." Another, from Holland, simply carried a photograph of Sir Winston pasted in the address space. A third had a drawing of the typical cigar between two fingers giving a V-for-Victory sign.

Many people gave flowers as presents. A riding school sent one of its smallest pupils in a pony and trap to deliver a huge bouquet of ninety red roses. A horticultural society in the West Indies raised the air fare to send one of its members with another bouquet. A number of small children knocked at the front door to hand in small posies of violets.

The messages of good will poured in nonstop. It must have been one of the most elaborate birthday card services ever organized by the G.P.O. The normally quiet cul-de-sac was constantly filled with a procession of callers and trucks which had to edge their way forward slowly through the crowds. The postmen delivered sacks of letters, parcels, and packets.

One of the telegrams was from a Nottinghamshire woman who was born at the same hour as Sir Winston.

Mr. Montague Browne was almost as excited as Sir Winston. "We're waist-deep in mail," he kept saying. The excitement mounted as the day went on. More cakes arrived, one having a brilliant portrait of Sir Winston in icing with a chocolate cigar in his mouth; another was a chocolate cake from the widow of Lord Beaverbrook. The iced inscription was in Latin and simple: "The Greatest."

A tub of Whitstable oysters was trundled down the hall to the kitchens for the family gathering that evening. Randolph Churchill arrived with flowers from his garden in East Bergholt, Suffolk. It must have been difficult to choose a present for a man who had everything, but his father liked flowers as much as anything.

He had shown a great interest in records over the previous year or so and found he enjoyed listening once more to melodies by Noel Coward and Gilbert and Sullivan.

He was given a stack of long-playing records. Lord Moran gave him a set of all the songs sung by the boys of Harrow School. Lady Birley gave a long-playing record of Gilbert and Sullivan selections. Mr. Montague Browne presented Sir Winston with a record of stirring military marches played by the Grenadier Guards.

During the afternoon the Harrow songs echoed round the bedroom as Sir Winston puffed contentedly at his cigar and continually nodded his appreciation of the good-will messages. He looked a picture of contentment, pleasantly surprised that he should be remembered by so many. It was not an act; he was quite sincere about it. He never took his popularity for granted and never looked bored by the continual admiration.

Lady Churchill's cousin, the Honourable Mrs. Sylvia Henley, a constant visitor to Hyde Park Gate and Chartwell, gave Sir Winston a handmade leopardskin muff to replace his old one, which was rather scarred by cigar burns. He always wore a muff when he sat in the garden; it had a small pocket on the inside that held a gasoline handwarmer. He used to wear out two muffs a year. He found gloves clumsy when he wanted to smoke his cigars and drink his whiskies and soda. Mrs. Henley was a regular card player in the Churchill household, often enjoying a game of bezique with Sir Winston after dinner.

One of the callers was Lord Moran, Sir Winston's old friend. He warmly shook Sir Winston's hand at his bedside and after leaving had this to say about his patient's spirit: "If you tell him he ought not to do something he will not listen, but, if you can convince him that it is to his advantage, he will always listen." I am not so sure that this was *always* strictly true.

In the kitchen Mrs. Douglas, the cook, headed a team of workers preparing the family dinner. Her day began at 7:30 A.M. when she prepared her menus and suggestions for the day, before taking them in to Lady Churchill at 8:30 A.M. after she had finished her breakfast in bed. Mrs. Douglas, author of two books, was a serious woman dedicated to her work in the kitchen. She was very pleasant, capable, and possibly the most efficient person on the staff.

She was a small Scottish woman with gray hair, very independent but most loyal. Her pet aversion was "intruders" in her kitchen.

In Sir Winston's bedroom, Randolph kissed his father on the cheek and wished him a happy birthday. At the same time the veterinary surgeon arrived to attend to Sir Winston's cat, Jock. It had an infected ear and had been under treatment for a week.

I took the vet into the bathroom to attend to the cat and he rubbed some ointment into its ear. Immediately released, it shot away into Sir Winston's bedroom, straight under his bed. It emerged only after the vet had gone, climbing up onto the bed and curling up to sleep at Sir Winston's feet.

Downstairs three waiters, specially hired for the day,

were helping the butler prepare the dining room for dinner while Lady Churchill supervised the arrangement of the flowers and worked out the seating positions for the guests. At six o'clock Lady Churchill went to her room for an hour's rest before the dinner party; she had had a busy day receiving the guests and organizing the household, but she looked as radiant as ever. She had a wonderful way as a hostess and no detail was too small for her attention.

Outside, people were still crowding the pavements, waiting for a glimpse of the evening callers as the street lights came on. There were nineteen for dinner. There should have been twenty but Lord Montgomery was ill in the hospital and could not attend. Round the family dining table with Sir Winston and Lady Churchill were their son, Randolph; his son Winston and his wife Minnie; Randolph's daughter, Arabella; Captain Christopher Soames and his wife Mary; Julian Sandys, son of Duncan Sandys and the late Mrs. Sandys (Diana Churchill); Celia Sandys, Julian's youngest sister; Mr. and Mrs. Piers Dixon; Lady Audley (actress Sarah Churchill); the then Mrs. Sylvia Henley; Mr. Jock Colville, and his wife, Lady Margaret Colville; and Mr. and Mrs. Montague Browne.

They sat down to a very special birthday menu of consomme, Whitstable oysters, partridge, ice cream and fruit, cheese and biscuits. At the dinner table Sir Winston was flanked by Sarah and Winston junior. Lady Churchill sat at the other end of the table, perfectly at ease giving a special secret smile to her husband during the meal. Over brandy, a toast was proposed to his health. Then Sir Winston cut his birthday cake. After three hours the ladies retired to the drawing room while Sir Winston and his male guests drank their brandies. A woodwind quartet of girl music students played "Happy Birthday," following it with a selection of Sir Winston's favorite songs including the Harrow School song, "Forty Years On."

The last guest left at 12:30 A.M., leaving Sir Winston sitting by the fire in the drawing room. He had thoroughly enjoyed every minute of his birthday. He remained for a quarter of an hour as the last of the logs burned out in the stone fireplace and finally went to bed at one o'clock, sleeping soundly the whole night.

The following day Sir Alec Douglas-Home, the ex-Premier, called to offer belated birthday greetings. He had intended paying his respects the day before but was held up by fog in Scotland.

The excitement of celebrating his ninetieth birthday tired Sir Winston out, and it showed over the next few days. No wonder! The staff were exhausted by the occasion; never had there been such activity at Hyde Park Gate. The days following were somewhat of an anticlimax. In fact, four days after the birthday when his dentist called, Sir Winston was very depressed. Remarkably enough, he still had most of his own teeth, but the dentist called from time to time for a check-up.

After examining his teeth, the dentist, Mr. Stewart-Ross, remarked that they were in good shape and would last "a while yet." Sir Winston looked straight at him and said, "I don't expect to live much longer, you know." It was a sad moment. I knew in my heart that he was right. Having reached ninety and no longer being a member of Parliament, he felt no further incentive remained in his life.

XXI

The End

Without doubt, Sir Winston's abiding love lay in the cut and thrust and unique atmosphere of the House of Commons. Although he realized that the break had come, giving up his seat at the general election in October 1964 was a great wrench.

With the pinnacle of his ninetieth birthday reached and passed in November, he became quiet and withdrawn. Those round him made every effort to interest and entertain him, but it seemed to everyone in the household that Sir Winston now felt he had little to look forward to.

He spent his time resting in bed each morning, and although he got up for lunch he became more and more reluctant to do so. In the afternoon he would sit in the drawing room staring into the fire. Occasionally he would read a book, but would only get through a chapter before laying it to one side. Even the press cuttings sent once a week by an agency failed to arouse his interest.

After tea he would retire to rest in his bedroom until dinner, which he had with Lady Churchill. Sometimes there were guests who managed to cheer him up for a while, but most evenings he appeared to be preoccupied with memories of bygone days. He was still smoking five or six cigars a day, taking one to his bedroom when he retired at midnight.

His ginger cat, Jock, gave him a lot of pleasure, sleeping on the bottom of his bed. He still read all the newspapers but less thoroughly than before. The family looked in during the day, bringing him small presents of flowers, a book, or cigars.

He was encouraged to watch more television, especially on Sunday afternoons when adventure films were shown.

The first real indication of what was to come was when he refused a cigar. I had never known him do this before. He would even light a cigar just before stepping into his bath. Looking back, it was the beginning of the end when the man and the symbol were parted.

He died, as the world knows, at his Hyde Park Gate home shortly after eight o'clock on the morning of Sunday, January 24th, 1965. Ten people were round his bed: six members of the family, Lord Moran, Mr. Montague Browne, Nurse Huddleston, and myself. The memory will remain with me for the rest of my life.

He had caught a chill after Christmas, but it was a mild one that gave no cause for alarm. Lord Moran was visiting him every Friday, and no one could possibly have had an idea that this cold was to lead to Sir Winston's death.

On the evening of Thursday, January 7th, he dined as usual with Lady Churchill in the sunken dining room. They had cold duck, French-fried potatoes and peas, and creme caramel. He drank a glass of champagne, followed by a brandy and cigar, before retiring to bed. But he could not sleep and spent a very restless night.

The next day he stayed in bed until evening, getting up for dinner, which he sat through in a very subdued mood. He did not say very much and when offered his cigar and brandy after the meal he said, quite emphatically, "No, I don't want it." He was even reluctant to go to bed. When he finally did go in the early hours of Saturday, January 9th, he was not to get up again.

That Sunday it was obvious that something was very wrong. Sir Winston had no appetite and was lethargic. The next day Lady Churchill was very distressed, and Lord Moran called in Lord Brain, the neurologist.

Sir Winston lay in his huge double bed on the ground floor and appeared to be in a very depressed state. On the table at his bedside lay his gold watch, the gold cigar case given him by Onassis, the gold clock given by Lord Beaverbrook, and a special copy of *This Island Race,* beautifully bound in red leather, a present from his publishers. Next to this was a pile of books from Kensington Public Library and a box of assorted cigars.

Lady Churchill and the family made every effort to try to lift him out of his depression. Flowers, specially brought from his Chartwell gardens, decorated the bedroom and were constantly being changed. Randolph and his son Winston called in, as did his daughter Mary. Sarah, Lady Audley, was abroad. She was informed that her father was not well, but it was not considered serious enough for her to fly straight back at that stage.

The bed was covered with a blue blanket, and at night a white counterpane, with hand-sewn raised red dots the size of sixpenny pieces, was put on. Three radiators in the bay window warmed the room, keeping it at a constant temperature of seventy degrees. When Sir Winston slept, the long flowered curtains were drawn at the window overlooking the garden. A green night light burned on the large writing desk in the corner.

Lord Moran called that Monday morning, later returning with Lord Brain. They arrived at the house at 5:30 P.M. and were received by Lady Churchill in the drawing room. She showed them into the bedroom and withdrew.

After a lengthy examination the two doctors returned to the drawing room and gently broke the news to her that Sir Winston had suffered a stroke.

That evening Mrs. Soames and her husband called to dine with Lady Churchill. All three spent some time at Sir Winston's bedside and were distressed when he did not appear to recognize them. His cat, Jock, still slept on the bottom of the bed, curled up in a ginger ball.

On Tuesday, January 12th, the effects of the stroke became very obvious. Sir Winston's left side had become paralyzed and he could only slightly move his left hand. He also had difficulty in focusing. He began to develop a bad cough and was put on a course of antibiotics.

He was putting up a tremendous fight, and the following two days his condition did not change. The news of the stroke was still kept secret. The family and Lord Moran decided this was the best course, because they knew that at the first mention of his illness an avalanche of sightseers would pack the quiet cul-de-sac outside.

On Thursday, January 14th, his condition was causing considerable anxiety. There had been no improvement, and this was bad. Mrs. Soames said she would stay at the house each night to help her mother, who was bearing up magnificently under the strain.

At this stage I had been on duty for eight consecutive nights and was due for a short rest. But Lady Churchill asked me to stay on. The entire arrangements for the nursing staff at the house were completely revised. Two nurses were to be on duty during the day, and two at night. I worked with Ann Huddleston, the tall twenty-three-year-old nurse from Yorkshire, who was excellent. She had been trained at St. George's Hospital and had been with Sir Winston a year. She was very popular with the family.

On the morning of Friday, January 15th, the two doctors, Lady Churchill, and Mrs. Soames had a long discussion in the drawing room. They knew that rumors about Sir Winston were already beginning to circulate and some had already reached Fleet Street. Mr. Montague Browne was authorized to make a statement to the press agencies saying that Sir Winston was not well "following a heavy cold." The headlines in the early editions of the London evening papers that Friday were, "Sir Winston Unwell." It was a tremendous understatement. But no one outside the Churchill family knew the real position.

Within an hour after the statement was made, the tiny Hyde Park Gate cul-de-sac was packed with newspapermen, photographers, and television teams. People passing by saw them and swelled the crowd. More than five hundred people were jammed round the front door when Lord Moran walked out of the house after lunch to read the first bulletin. He stood on the pavement and read from a slip of paper, "After a cold, Sir Winston has developed a circulatory weakness and there has been a cerebral thrombosis."

Immediately a buzz ran through the crowd, "He's had a stroke . . . old Winnie's had a stroke." At last the true position was being made clear. But from now on there was to be added strain on the family because we were literally in a state of siege. High arc lights shone on the front door whenever anyone entered or left the house, television cables lay across the pavement, despatch riders constantly revved their motorcycles as they waited for pictures to be rushed back to newspaper offices, a mobile canteen was set up at the end of the street, television commentators seemed to be continually recording or perhaps rehearsing their on-the-spot reports. A Salvation Army band asked if they could play hymns outside the house. They were thanked and reluctantly turned down.

Lord Moran's second bulletin that day said that there had been little change in Sir Winston's condition but that he was "slipping into deeper sleep" and was "not conscious of pain or discomfort."

Scores of telegrams were arriving by the hour, and many people brought flowers. An elderly woman leaving a bunch of daffodils said, "Be sure you put them in water and make sure you give him my love."

Lady Churchill, sitting in her first-floor bedroom, put through a call to Sarah in Rome. She told her the seriousness of the position and advised her to fly home immediately. The Queen, staying at Sandringham, was kept informed. The Prime Minister, Mr. Harold Wilson, called on his way to Chequers.

Sarah flew in and drove straight home, arriving at the house shortly after two o'clock on the Saturday morning. Her mother was in bed after a particularly trying day. Mary had waited up for her sister and gave her coffee in the drawing room after Sarah had seen her father. She was very tired after the flight, which had been delayed five hours. The jetliner she had caught in Rome had turned back with electrical trouble, and she had to catch a second plane. She sat at the bedside in an armchair and held her father's hand, remaining with him for some time.

Lord Moran called as usual, and when he left a reporter asked him if Sir Winston was unconscious. He refused to comment. He knew his patient had been semi-comatose for the last three days but did not want to spread alarm and despondency.

That night hope flickered briefly when Sir Winston appeared to be slightly improving. He seemed to recognize the voices of his visitors and managed to drink some glucose and orange juice. His temperature was down to normal and a wave of optimism swept through the house. It was not to last long.

By the morning of Monday, January 18th, the situation was very different. And at 2:30 A.M. the next day, when

Sir Winston's breathing became erratic, Lord Moran was called from his bed. He arrived at the house, slipped off his overcoat and white silk scarf, and hurried into the bedroom. After examining Sir Winston he talked to Lady Churchill and her daughter and advised against calling the family to the house at that stage. Although Sir Winston responded to treatment in the early hours, there was little doubt that death was not many days away and Lord Moran had to tell the reporters that his patient had "lost ground." He decided to stay at the house that night, snatching a few hours sleep in an armchair.

Each day the routine was the same. Lord Moran called, examined his patient, talked to Lady Churchill in her bedroom to decide on the wording of the bulletin, which he then read on the doorstep to the pressmen who were keeping a round-the-clock vigil. Lady Churchill's room was immediately above the front door and the television arc lights directly faced it. Each night when she retired she could undoubtedly hear the crowd outside. With the continual strain of the glaring lights, the crowds and the noise, she eventually asked Mr. Montague Browne to request the crowd to withdraw. This they did within minutes, and Lady Churchill sent a special word of appreciation to the pressmen who had the difficult and delicate task of covering the house.

It was typical of her courage that she did not move into a quieter bedroom. She stuck it out for four days before deciding to make her request. She was only three months away from her eightieth birthday and was under tremendous strain. Her doctor was visiting her throughout to ensure she did not tax herself too much. Her whole bearing at the time was both dignified and restrained, and the emotion she must have felt was kept for the privacy of her room. The household staff, the crowds outside, and the whole world marveled at her courage.

Four secretaries in the office were kept busy dealing with all the inquiries. They often told callers the time of the next bulletin or simply repeated the last one. Randolph stayed throughout at the nearby Hyde Park Hotel; his son remained at his London flat. Mary Soames continued to comfort her mother, sometimes personally helping with her father.

Outside the house the pavements were deserted, but a small crowd of people stood at the end of the street. Among them was a bearded New Zealand sailor called Bob Wilson, who slept each night in a doorway rather than give up his vigil. From time to time he knelt in silent prayer, and many prayers were said by that small congregation.

Before the crowd was moved away from the house, few could have realized that they were within earshot of Sir Winston's bedroom. As the doctors and nurses sat in the small ante-room, fronting onto the street, they could hear the hubbub outside. Occasionally they peeped through the curtain at the crowd. It is difficult to describe the tremendous relief felt by everyone in the house when the crowd withdrew. It was as if a great pressure had been relieved.

Sir Winston, propped up with a dozen pillows and wearing a green bed jacket, slipped deeper and deeper into unconsciousness. I tried to remember the last time he had spoken but was unable to do so. His last words were probably to make some quite innocuous remark.

As he sat upright, his head was supported by a small soft pillow, and he looked to be in a peaceful sleep. Every member of the family called at some time during the day, and there were also visits from close friends.

On Friday, January 22nd, Lady Churchill had a phone call from Sir Winston's grandson, Winston. He told her that his wife, Minnie, had given birth to a baby son in the Westminster Hospital. Although the family was overjoyed to hear that the baby, born prematurely, and mother were well, their joy was overshadowed by the fact that it was certain that Sir Winston, who loved children, would never see his great-grandson.

The next day everyone in the house was conscious of the fact that it was the eve of the seventy-first anniversary of the death of Sir Winston's father, Lord Randolph Churchill. Nothing was said, but the same thought was in everyone's mind. And that is how it was.

That night the family retired to bed, giving instructions that we were to call them should there be any change. Mrs. Soames, the last to go to her bedroom, visited her father shortly after midnight.

Lady Churchill, who used to get up during the night to visit her husband, came down at her usual time, just after one o'clock. She held her husband's hand, stayed with him for a few minutes, and then returned upstairs. Nurse Huddleston and I took turns sitting at the bedside for the rest of the dark hours.

It was about five o'clock when Mrs. Soames returned, as she had done every morning during the illness. There had been a change, and the three of us held a brief conference. It was decided that it would be better to let Lady Churchill get as much rest as possible so she was not called.

She came down a few minutes before seven and talked to Mrs. Soames in the bedroom. They agreed to inform close members of the family. Mrs. Soames telephoned from the morning room, also calling Lord Moran and Mr. Montague Browne.

Half an hour later the front doorbell rang, and Randolph and his son, Winston, arrived with Sarah, Lady Audley; Celia Sandys; Lord Moran; and the secretary. They all went straight into the bedroom and then retired to the drawing room. Nurse Huddleston took them in a tray of coffee and hot milk. No one spoke.

It was now the final act. I went into the room where the

family was gathered and said, "I think you had all better come in." My voice was a little hoarse and I had to repeat myself. They came in one by one to join Lady Churchill and Mrs. Soames, already kneeling at either side of Sir Winston's bed. Slowly the others sank to their knees around the room.

He died a few minutes later, quite peacefully.

Farewell

Six days later I attended the State Funeral Service in St. Paul's Cathedral. As I stood there I felt a great emptiness, the legend had been so real for me.

Nurse Felicity Leeming, from Guernsey, and Nurse Adrienne Knox, a New Zealander, who had been the other half of the nursing team, stood with Ann Huddleston and myself just below the South Arch. Around us was a sea of famous faces. All of us felt a sense of loss, too personal to share even with each other. Memories flooded back as the world paid tribute . . . his courage . . . his humor . . . his pugnacity . . . his great love of people . . . his great love of life.

> *"The oldest among us can recall*
> *nothing to compare with it and*
> *the younger ones among you,*
> *however long you live, will never*
> *see the like again."*

Index